# COWGIRL

## G. R. Gemin

*Adapted by* Mike Kenny

Teaching and Learning
activities written by
Paul Bunyan and Ruth Moore

OXFORD
UNIVERSITY PRESS

# OXFORD
### UNIVERSITY PRESS

Great Clarendon Street, Oxford, OX2 6DP,
United Kingdom

Oxford University Press is a department of the University of Oxford.
It furthers the University's objective of excellence in research, scholarship,
and education by publishing worldwide. Oxford is a registered trade mark of Oxford
University Press in the UK and in certain other countries

British Library Cataloguing in Publication Data
Data available

ISBN 978-0-19-836715-4

1 3 5 7 9 10 8 6 4 2

Printed in Great Britain by Bell and Bain Ltd., Glasgow

**Acknowledgements**
The publisher and author are grateful for permission to reprint the following
copyright material:

Extracts from G. R. Gemin: *Cowgirl* (Nosy Crow, 2014), copyright © G. R Gemin 2014.

Cover image: BMG/Shutterstock
Artwork on page 89 by Giorgio Bacchin

The Publisher would like to thank Ruth Moore and Paul Bunyan for writing the
Activities section.

# CONTENTS

# WHAT THE ADAPTER SAYS

At the heart of *Cowgirl* is a herd of cows. Now you might think that that presents an impossible challenge for a playwright. I wouldn't be surprised if you did. But, honestly? That sort of thing is mother's milk to those of us who write for the stage. I'll let you down slowly. There will not be real cows wandering around in any production of this play. It's impossible. To tell the truth, I'm not even sure that is legal. However, you will see cows. I guarantee it.

Even the most realistic of productions is never actually real. It's the job of the theatre to make you see things that aren't actually there. It requires you to awaken your imagination. This goes back to Shakespeare and beyond. If we can do the battle of Agincourt and Hamlet's father's ghost, a herd of cows should be a piece of cake.

To be honest, in adapting *Cowgirl* for performance, the cows were never the problem. I loved the book. I cared about the people in it. I was moved, and occasionally I laughed out loud, but it wasn't easy to contain the raucous energy of it on a stage. It has a huge canvas. It is about a community and I had to combine a few members of it in order to make it work. Read the book as well. There is a wealth of lovely detail and characters I had to lose in putting it on the stage. Hopefully they complement each other.

This is a piece with strong themes of relationships in families and a community, but its beating heart is a growing friendship between two girls. That doesn't normally get much of an airing on our stages, so it makes it something special and rare, and in this case that friendship is drawn so well. They're both strong characters, at some points vulnerable, but most importantly, Gemma and Kate feel real.

*Mike Kenny*

# WHAT THE AUTHOR SAYS

Writing for the theatre, in my opinion, is the most difficult of the writing disciplines. So it was especially flattering and satisfying when OUP wanted to adapt *Cowgirl* for the stage.

When I set out to write *Cowgirl* I knew it would not just be about Gemma, but a community of people of all ages. A community affected collectively and individually, but ultimately a community that could change collectively and individually.

From the beginning of the adaptation process with Mike Kenny it was clear to me that 'the community' was at the core of the adaptation. Beyond that it needed the vision of a writer who understood the confines and creative possibilities of the stage. The play and the book are separate entities. They have to be. What Mike has written is fundamentally for the theatre (notwithstanding the challenging inclusion of a herd of dairy cows).

When I wrote *Cowgirl*, I hoped that Gemma would speak to the reader and connect with them; I hoped her indifference to cows, which develops into a positive obsession, would surprise and touch people, and I wish the same for Mike Kenny's adaptation – a whole community is depending on it!

*Giancarlo Gemin*

# CHARACTER LIST

Gemma, *a 13-year-old girl*
Kate, *a physically imposing 13-year-old girl who lives on a farm*
Gran, *Gemma's grandmother*
Mam, *Gemma's mother*
Dad, *Gemma's father*
Darren, *Gemma's brother*
Mr Thomas, *Kate's father*
Jamie, Ryan and Sian, *local teenagers*
Mr Banerjee, *Gran's next door neighbour*
Karuna, *Mr Banerjee's 15-year-old grandson*
Roger, Mave and Morris, *Gran's neighbours*
Mostyn, *a local farmer*
Jane and Donna, *special cows in the herd*

The chorus
*A herd of 12 cows, residents of the Bryn Mawr Estate, the schoolchildren.*
Teacher; Policeman; Bike man; John, Mary and children; Man from estate with children; Mr Jarvis and Mrs Conway; Mr Llewellyn; Mr and Mrs Evans; Girl and Boy; Woman.

# ACT ONE

● ● ● ● ● ● ● ● ● ● ● ● ● ● ● ● ● ● ● ● ● ● ● ● ● ● ● ● ● ● ● ● ● ● ● ● ● ● ● ● ● ● ● ● ● ●

**SCENE 1**

*The whole cast look at the audience. They slowly begin to transform into cattle, chewing the cud: a swish of a tail, a stamp of a foot, a twitch of an ear. They begin to moo and then they cohere into a herd, jostling. They are a herd, and become a choir of mooing.*

*Cutting across this comes **Gemma**, on her bike, peddling and screaming.*

**Gemma**   *[To the audience]* So, I'm on my bike, coming down Craig-y-Nos and, all right, I do have my eyes closed.

Aaaaaaaaaaaaaah!

*More mooing.*

Aaaaaaaaaaaaaah! Cows!

*She crashes into them, falling head over heels. The bike going one way, the cows scattering, she hits the ground. Silence. The cows start to gather around her.*

**Cow**   Moo.

**Gemma**   *[Screams]* Aaaaaah! Get away from me. Get away.

**Cow**   Moo.

**Gemma**   Aaaaaah! Get away.

**Kate**   *[Emerging from the herd]* Shut up! What are you screeching about? You're scaring them.

**Gemma**   I know who you are! You're Cowgirl! Get 'em away! Get 'em away from me!

**Kate**   They're cows. Cows, not crocodiles. They won't do you any harm. *[She claps her hands]* Come on girls. Jane. Rachel. Donna.

5

| **Gemma** | They're scared of you, see. They're not scared of me. |
| **Kate** | Oh yeah? Megan, away! |
| **Gemma** | They shouldn't be on the road. |
| **Kate** | They're dairy cows. They're not bulls. There's a difference. You were going too fast. And you had your eyes shut. *[She looks at **Gemma**'s leg]* You've hurt your leg. |
| **Gemma** | It's all right. I gotta go. My gran… |
| **Kate** | You should clean up those cuts. I've got to get these to the barn. |
| | ***Kate** goes with the cows.* |
| **Gemma** | *[To the audience]* Well, what could I do? I followed her. |

• • • • • • • • • • • • • • • • • • • • • • • • • • • • • • • • • • • • • • • •

**SCENE 2**

*The barn.*

| **Gemma** | What you doing? |
| **Kate** | What's it look like?! |
| **Gemma** | Milking. |
| **Kate** | Yeah well, that's what I'm doing. |
| **Gemma** | Oh. |
| **Kate** | It doesn't start in cartons, you know. You never seen milking before? |
| **Gemma** | Yeah. Course I have. On the telly. |
| | ***Kate** continues to milk the cows while **Gemma** watches.* |
| **Kate** | There's water over there. You can wash your cuts clean. |
| | ***Mr Thomas**, Kate's dad, comes in.* |
| **Mr Thomas** | *[Stressed]* Kate! You still milking? *[Looking at **Gemma**]* Who's this? |

| | |
|---|---|
| **Gemma** | I'm Gemma. |
| | *It seems to need more explanation and **Kate** is saying nothing.* |
| | From school. |
| **Kate** | She hurt her leg. |
| **Mr Thomas** | *[To **Gemma**]* Not gonna sue us, are you? *[Turns back to **Kate**]* I need to talk to you. |
| **Kate** | I can't rush 'em, Dad. |
| | ***Mr Thomas** goes. **Kate** returns to milking.* |
| **Kate** | Still scared? |
| **Gemma** | No. |
| **Kate** | You wanna try? Put the suckers on. |
| **Gemma** | I gotta get back. |
| **Kate** | Go then. |
| **Gemma** | I will. |
| | ***Gemma**'s phone rings.* |
| | *[Under her breath]* Rude cow. *[On the phone]* Mam? |
| | ***Mam** enters.* |
| **Mam** | *[On the phone]* Gemma, where are you? |
| **Gemma** | Out on my bike. |
| **Mam** | Your gran needs you. |
| **Gemma** | Why? What's happened? |
| **Mam** | Ruby's dead. |
| **Gemma** | Is that all? |
| **Mam** | You are heartless sometimes, Gemma. You know how much your gran loved that dog. |
| **Gemma** | What am I supposed to do about it? |

| Mam | I said you'd go round and bury it for her. |
| Gemma | Me?! Mam, you and Darren are nearer. |
| Mam | OK, Gemma, I'll go, shall I? And you can get back here and make dinner with your brother then? This is your gran's dog we're talking about. But never you mind, I'll do it… |

*Mam leaves.*

| Gemma | All right, all right. I'll go. *[To Kate]* I gotta go. |
| Kate | See you. Eh? |
| Gemma | What? |
| Kate | Cowgirl. I like that. |

*Gemma leaves.*

• • • • • • • • • • • • • • • • • • • • • • • • • • • • • • • • • • • • • • • • • • • • • • •

**SCENE 3**

*Our chorus turn into the population of the Bryn Mawr Estate.* **Gemma** *is pushing her bike through. She comes to* **Gran's** *house. It's pouring with rain.*

| Gemma | *[To the audience]* I'd been in the countryside, but you have to cross a bridge to Bryn Mawr Estate. It's another world. You don't want to live here, I tell you. There's a new bit and an old bit. My gran lives in the old bit. |
| Gran | Oh now, look at this. You brought the weather with you. Half an hour ago it was just spitting. At least it will make the digging easier. Silver lining, see. Every cloud. Here's the shovel. |
| Gemma | You not going to let me in? |
| Gran | Well, you're not going to get any wetter, are you? And I don't want you traipsing too much mud in the house. |

*Gemma starts to dig.*

| Gran | Make sure there's a big enough hole. It's got to take the shrub too. |

8

| | |
|---|---|
| **Gemma** | Yes, Gran. *[Under her breath]* The only one who liked you was Gran, because she was the only one who you didn't snarl at or bite. |
| | *Mr Banerjee is watching.* |
| **Gemma** | Do you want something? |
| **Mr Banerjee** | Dog dead? |
| **Gemma** | Yeah. Hope so. I'm burying her. |
| | *Mr Banerjee leaves as Jamie enters.* |
| **Jamie** | S'up Gemma? |
| **Gemma** | Burying Ruby. |
| **Jamie** | Cool. |
| **Gran** | *[To Jamie]* Get *away*. Go on. Chopsing in my yard. |
| **Jamie** | Bit me once, that dog did. Had to have a jab. |
| **Gemma** | Yeah, I remember – Ruby hated having that jab. |
| **Jamie** | No, me – I had the jab. |
| **Gran** | Get away, you little hoodie. |
| **Jamie** | Not wearing a hood. |
| | *Gran grabs the shovel.* |
| **Gran** | You get or I'll be digging a bigger hole, you little— |
| | *Gran threatens him with the shovel.* |
| **Jamie** | *[Dodging away]* Glad your dog's dead. |
| | *Jamie runs off.* |
| **Gran** | *[To Gemma]* Just stand there why don't you! |
| **Gemma** | He's not worth it, Gran. |
| **Gran** | I can't even bury Ruby in peace. And poor Mave, down the terrace, getting burgled only yesterday while she was in her own home… This place is going to Hell! |

*Gran goes and brings back a bundle.* **Mr Banerjee** *returns.*

| | |
|---|---|
| **Gemma** | *[Reaches for it]* Let me. |
| **Gran** | No, I want to do it. |

*Mr Banerjee puts some flowers on the bundle.*

| | |
|---|---|
| **Mr Banerjee** | For your dog's soul. |
| **Gran** | Thank you, Mr Banerjee. |

*They bury the dog, and place the flowers on top. A moment. They hear beautiful flute music.* **Gemma** *looks up. She can't quite believe it's real.*

| | |
|---|---|
| **Mr Banerjee** | My grandson. He's in his bedroom playing the flute. |

*Mr Banerjee leaves.*

| | |
|---|---|
| **Gemma** | Oh. Gran, I better be going. |
| **Gran** | Come on. Stay and have something to eat with me. |
| **Gemma** | You sure? |
| **Gran** | Yeah. For me. You gotta keep busy. |
| **Gemma** | You always say that. |
| **Gran** | If you don't keep busy, you'll fade and die. |

• • • • • • • • • • • • • • • • • • • • • • • • • • • • • • • • • • • • • • • •

## SCENE 4

*The kitchen.*

| | |
|---|---|
| **Gran** | Here. Dry yourself and put on one of your grandad's old jumpers. |
| **Gemma** | Need any help? |
| **Gran** | Sit. |

*Gran busies herself.*

It's getting worse on the Bryn Mawr.

| | |
|---|---|
| **Gemma** | What happened to Mave then? |

| | |
|---|---|
| **Gran** | Burgled in her own home. She answers her front door and there's this boy asking for odd jobs. Keeps her talking. She hears a crash indoors. Catches these boys red-handed. They got away with her jar of pound coins. |
| **Gemma** | Terrible. |
| **Gran** | We all go down the post office as a mob to get our pensions. This estate is ugly, like it's a war zone. We're all scared on this terrace. Like prisoners in our own homes. |
| | *They hear the flute again.* |
| **Gemma** | They're a bit weird. Next door. |
| **Gran** | The Banerjees? They're lovely people. They look out for each other, and me – more than my own daughter. |
| **Gemma** | I'm here, aren't I? |
| **Gran** | When was the last time you all came round? |
| **Gemma** | Last Sunday. |
| **Gran** | No. Sunday before. |
| **Gemma** | Oh. |
| | *Silence.* |
| | I hate cows. |
| **Gran** | What's a cow ever done to you? |
| **Gemma** | I was out on my bike up by Craig-y-Nos. |
| **Gran** | What were you doing up there? |
| **Gemma** | Oh, nothing. Just looking for somewhere. Anyway, these cows attacked me. Knocked me off. Were gonna trample me to death. Suddenly Cowgirl comes from nowhere— |
| **Gran** | Who? |
| **Gemma** | Weird girl at school. Cowgirl, we call her. Huge and scary, like her cows. |
| **Gran** | Cows won't harm you. |

| Gemma | That's what she said. |
|---|---|
| Gran | What's this girl's name? |
| Gemma | Kate Thomas. |
| Gran | I knew her grandfather. |
| Gemma | You never. |
| Gran | When I was a land girl in the war. I was scared of cows too at first, but I had no choice. There was a farm worker a few years older than us girls. Strong, hardly said a word. Us girls all fancied him. |
| Gemma | Gran! |
| Gran | Gareth Thomas. Your Kate's granddad, I bet. Tell you what, invite Kate round here for lunch. |
| Gemma | No way, Gran! Nobody likes her. |
| Gran | I just buried my Ruby. And I don't ask much of you. |
| Gemma | But I don't know her, Gran. |
| Gran | You're scared of her, aren't you? |
| Gemma | No. |
| Gran | She's just a girl, Gemma, like you. I like the sound of her. Lunch. Day after tomorrow. You'll invite her and that's that. |
| Gemma | Great. Totally fab'lous. |
| | *Gran leaves.* |

● ● ● ● ● ● ● ● ● ● ● ● ● ● ● ● ● ● ● ● ● ● ● ● ● ● ● ● ● ● ● ● ● ● ● ● ● ● ● ●

**SCENE 5**

*Immediately into* **Gemma***'s home.* **Mam** *and* **Darren** *are there.*

| Gemma | *[To the audience]* So I goes home. |
|---|---|
| Mam | Where you been? |
| Gemma | Gran's. You told me to. |

| | |
|---|---|
| **Mam** | Till now? |
| **Gemma** | Mam! What d'you expect? Bury Ruby and go? |
| **Darren** | How long's it take to bury a dog? |
| **Gemma** | Shut up, Darren. |
| **Darren** | She was with her boyfriend. |
| **Gemma** | I haven't got a boyfriend! |
| **Mam** | What's this? What boyfriend? |
| **Darren** | Nobody'd have her. |
| **Gemma** | I haven't got a boyfriend! |
| **Mam** | Did she say she was getting another dog? |
| **Gemma** | She's just buried Ruby. |
| **Mam** | Well, I hope she doesn't. |
| **Gemma** | Why? |
| **Mam** | Does it not cross your mind that since your father has been inside, like the plank he is, I need all the help I can get? I don't want your gran throwing her money away on another animal. |
| **Gemma** | Why, cos you want it? |
| **Mam** | What did you say? |
| **Darren** | She said, 'Cos you want it!', Mam. |
| **Mam** | Don't you ever give me that lip, Gemma. |
| **Darren** | Yeah! |
| **Gemma** | [*Goes for him*] Darren! You shut your nasty, stirring gob. |
| **Mam** | Gemma! |
| **Darren** | Mam! |

**Darren** *grabs the Tom Jones statue.*

Mam! Look out, Gemma! You'll break Dad's Tom Jones statue.

| Mam | Leave him be, Gemma. |
| Gemma | I'm fed up of your creeping, your greasy hair, your disgusting pants on the bathroom floor. A rat's cleaner than you are. |
| Darren | Mam! Get her off! |
| Mam | Gemma! Tom Jones! |
| Gemma | …The way you slurp your cereal, your finger always up your nose in front of the telly. |
| Mam | That's enough. Careful. |

*The Tom Jones statue drops and smashes. They pause.*

| Darren | Now look what you've done! |
| Gemma | I've had it with him. |
| Darren | She's a nutter! |
| Mam | Stop! Your dad loved that Tom Jones. |
| Darren | You'll have to tell him next visiting time. |
| Mam | Why are you always fighting, eh? |
| Darren | It's not unusual. |
| Gemma | Shut up. It takes two to fight, Mam. |
| Mam | I don't know what's got into you, Gemma, honest to God I don't, but go to your room now. Go on! |
| Darren | [As **Gemma** goes] She's proper mad, isn't she, Mam? |

*Mam and Darren leave.*

| Gemma | Creep. |

## SCENE 6

*Gemma in her room. She gets out a box.*

**Gemma**   *[To the audience]* All right, you're not to laugh. When I was on my bike I was looking for somewhere, but I didn't find it. It was a waterfall. Dad took us there for a picnic. Dad and Darren dared each other to put their heads in the icy water. I was wearing these new sandals Dad had bought me and they got all dirty. It was a few days after that he got arrested. Mam was crying. I was crying. It was horrible. He said he'd be back, but he wasn't. They sent him to prison for petty larceny and fraud, which is a posh way of saying cheating and stealing.

Well, the day after he was arrested I was putting on my new shoes and I noticed dried grass and leaves stuck to the soles. I cried. Again. Not because they were all dirty but because that was the last day everything was OK. I put the mud and leaves in this box. Just dirt, people'd say. And I just feel like, if I could find it. Go back to that place…

*Gemma puts the box away.*

## SCENE 7

**Gemma**   *[To the audience]* Back to reality. Next morning. On the way to school.

*Sian arrives.*

**Sian**   Hiya, Gem.

**Gemma**   Hiya, Sian.

**Sian**   How's it going?

**Gemma**   Yeah, good.

**Sian**   Your dad still inside, is he?

**Gemma**   *[Wishing Sian wouldn't mention it]* Yeah.

| Sian | That's cool, that is. I wish my dad was. Look at her. Cowgirl. *[To **Kate**]* Where are your cows, girl? |
| | ***Kate*** *ignores this. Others laugh.* |
| | OK. How are your girls, Cow? |
| | ***Kate*** *looks at **Gemma**.* |
| Gemma | *[Gets up]* Come on, Sian. |
| Sian | Wait. *[To **Kate**]* Hey, Cowgirl. I don't like being ignored. |
| Kate | We'll be late for school. |
| | ***Kate*** *tries to pass **Sian**. **Sian** blocks her way. **Sian** pushes her.* |
| | You gonna let me past? |
| | ***Sian*** *doesn't move.* |
| | All right then. |
| | ***Kate*** *swiftly bends down and lifts **Sian** over her shoulder.* |
| Sian | Put me down, you cow! |
| Kate | Thanks for the compliment. |
| | *The crowd gathers around trying to get **Kate** to put **Sian** down. **Gemma** is on the edge of it. **Kate** just pushes through. A **teacher** arrives.* |
| Teacher | What's going on? |
| Kate | I was worried we were going to be late, Sir. |
| Teacher | Come on, now, put her down. |
| | ***Kate*** *puts **Sian** down. **Sian** takes a swing for **Kate**. **Kate** grabs **Sian**'s arm and twists it.* |
| | That's enough. Now, what's all this about? |
| Sian | She's a cow. |
| Kate | Bit ungrateful, don't you think, Sir? I made sure she didn't miss her first lesson and this is all the thanks I get. |

| | |
|---|---|
| **Teacher** | All right now. Get to registration. |
| **Sian** | Sir?! |
| **Teacher** | Now. |

*Everyone goes, leaving **Kate** and **Gemma**.*

| | |
|---|---|
| **Kate** | What? |
| **Gemma** | My gran wants you to come to lunch tomorrow. |
| **Kate** | Excuse me? |
| **Gemma** | My gran wants you to come to lunch tomorrow. |
| **Kate** | Why? |
| **Gemma** | Dunno. |
| **Kate** | How does she know me? |
| **Gemma** | I told her about your cows. She used to be a thingy during the war – worked on a farm… |
| **Kate** | Land girl? |
| **Gemma** | That's it. Well? |
| **Kate** | No thanks. Ask Sian. |
| **Gemma** | She hasn't got cows, has she? My gran won't believe I asked you if you don't. |
| **Kate** | Why should I? |
| **Gemma** | You both like cows, there's free food and her dog just died. Please? |
| **Kate** | OK. As long as you walk there and back with me. |
| **Gemma** | Whatever. |
| **Kate** | School entrance, half twelve tomorrow. |

***Kate** leaves.*

## SCENE 8

*At **Gran's**. **Gemma**, **Kate** and **Gran** are there.*

**Gemma**    *[To the audience]* I didn't think she'd turn up, but she's a woman of her word.

**Gran**    Kate, right?

**Kate**    That's right.

**Gran**    Call me Lilly. I used to know your grandad. In the war.

**Kate**    Gemma said.

**Gran**    Gareth.

**Kate**    Yeah!

**Gran**    Ooh, he was handsome. Big too. Built like a brick… well you know.

**Kate**    I take after him. And with the cows.

**Gran**    I used to do the milking, up early. Freezing in the winter. I expect it's all changed now.

**Kate**    Still have to get up early.

**Gran**    No, they won't wait, cows. How many you got?

**Kate**    Twelve. We used to have more, but…

**Gran**    I used to talk to them while I milked them. Sing to them too.

**Gemma**    Gran?!

*__Roger__ suddenly shouts.*

**Roger**    Lilly! Lilly! We got them this time.

**Gran**    *[Getting up]* Come on you two.

*__Roger__ brings in __Jamie__ and __Ryan__.*

**Roger**    They tried it again. Like with Mave.

**Gemma**    It's Jamie and Ryan. Sian's brother.

| | |
|---|---|
| **Gran** | You know 'em? |
| **Roger** | One round the front ringing the doorbell. Found these two in my lounge, rifling around. Call the police for me. |
| | *Others are gathering.* |
| **Gran** | Oh, this place has gone rotten. |
| **Jamie** | We did nothing. |
| **Ryan** | Zero to nick anyway. |
| **Mave** | What's going on, Lilly? |
| **Gran** | Roger caught these two in his house. |
| **Neighbour** | Oh, that's twice this week! |
| | ***Ryan** struggles and runs, but is caught by **Kate**.* |
| **Ryan** | Our Sian'll kill you when I tell her. |
| **Kate** | That supposed to make me let you go, is it? |
| **Jamie** | Get her off, Gemma. |
| **Gemma** | Go on. Let 'em go. |
| **Gran and Roger** | What? NO! |
| **Gran** | It's all right, is it, Gemma? These boys – and girls too – making our lives a misery. The Bryn Mawr Estate was a lovely place years ago when they first built it. My back door was always open. |
| **Roger** | That's right. |
| **Mr Banerjee** | A community. |
| **Gran** | Aye. Those days are well gone now. The doors are double bolted and we don't go out after dark. It's horrible, Gemma, and it makes me glad to be at the end of my life rather than at the beginning. |
| | ***Darren** appears on the edge of the crowd.* |
| **Roger** | That's the monkey that rang my doorbell! |

| | |
|---|---|
| **Gemma** | Darren! |
| **Gran** | Come here. |
| **Darren** | They made me do it, Gran. |
| **Gemma** | You wait till I tell Mam! |
| **Gran** | Oh I see. Changed your tune now it's your own brother that's involved. |
| **Gemma** | I can't win! |
| **Gran** | He's my neighbour, Darren. Not that it makes it right if he wasn't. What d'you think they were doing round the back while you rang the bell? |
| **Darren** | It was just a laugh. |
| **Gran** | My own flesh and blood. |
| | *Kate slings Ryan over her shoulder.* |
| **Ryan** | NO! Put me down! |
| **Kate** | I think I can manage that one too. |
| | *Kate gets Jamie on the other shoulder.* |
| | Thanks for lunch, Lilly. |
| **Gran** | Pleasure's all mine. |
| **Kate** | And if you want to come up the farm and practise your milking some time, you'd be very welcome. |
| **Gran** | I'd love to. |
| **Gemma** | You can't. |
| **Gran** | Why ever not? |
| **Gemma** | How would you get up there? |
| **Mr Banerjee** | I'll take you, Lilly. I like cows too. |
| **Gran** | Well there we are then, Kate. You're a star. |
| **Gemma** | *[Ironically]* Happy days. |

## SCENE 9

*The crowd fades away. Some of the chorus become school children.* ***Jamie*** *and* ***Ryan*** *are still struggling on* ***Kate's*** *shoulders.*

| | |
|---|---|
| **Kate** | See those stingy nettles? You do that again and I'll walk backwards through them. |
| **Jamie** | I feel sick. |
| **Ryan** | PUT US DOWN! |

*Sian arrives.*

| | |
|---|---|
| **Sian** | Put my brother down! |
| **Kate** | Not yet. Almost there. |
| **Sian** | *[To* ***Gemma]*** Why didn't you stop her? |
| **Ryan** | She was with her, Sian. She was there. |
| **Gemma** | I was sorting my brother out, wasn't I? |
| **Darren** | They were round my gran's. |
| **Sian** | Cosy. You are in deep trouble. Put 'em down – now! |
| **Kate** | No! |
| **Gemma** | You gotta be kidding! |
| **Kate** | Do I look like I'm kidding?! |

*Sian and her friends grab* ***Jamie*** *and* ***Ryan***. *There is a struggle. The watchers – the other schoolchildren – are laughing.* ***Gemma*** *is anxious. Finally they end up in a heap.*

Oh dear. See you, then.

| | |
|---|---|
| **Gemma** | *[To* ***Darren]*** You wait till I tell Mam. |
| **Darren** | I never knew what they were doing! |
| **Gemma** | You're a liar. |

| **Darren** | And she won't believe you, anyway. |
| | ***Sian***, ***Jamie***, ***Ryan***, ***Darren*** *and the other schoolchildren leave.* |

• • • • • • • • • • • • • • • • • • • • • • • • • • • • • • • • • • • • • • • • • • •

**SCENE 10**

| | ***Kate**'s farm.* ***Kate*** *is hosing the floor. She is singing in Welsh.* |
| **Gemma** | *[To the audience]* She believed me. She just never did nothing about it. Anyway, the next week, I'm on my bike again, back over the bridge and riding up to Cowgirl's farm. |
| **Kate** | *[Taken by surprise]* Shouldn't creep up on people! |
| **Gemma** | Sorry. |
| **Kate** | Lilly here? |
| **Gemma** | No. I came on my bike. |
| **Kate** | I'll go and get Jane. |
| **Gemma** | That your mam? |
| **Kate** | She's a cow. |
| **Gemma** | What? Your mam? |
| **Kate** | No! Jane. Jane is a cow, you stupid– |
| **Gemma** | You invited my gran, you did. You didn't invite me, but she's my gran… and I want her to have a nice day. |
| **Kate** | I'll get Jane. You wait here for your gran. |
| | ***Kate*** *leaves.* ***Gran*** *arrives.* |
| **Gemma** | Hiya Gran. |
| | ***Gemma*** *sees* ***Mr Banerjee*** *behind* ***Gran***. |
| | What's he doing here? |
| **Gran** | Gemma, do me a favour. I've been looking forward to today so don't show us up. He's come to see the cow, like me. And |

22

as a Hindu he has more right to be here than us. Isn't that right, Mr Banerjee? The cow is a special animal in India.

**Mr Banerjee**   Very special. Sacred.

*Mr Thomas arrives.*

**Mr Thomas**   Like Cardiff Central in here today. You all come to see Kate?

**Gran**   Yes. She invited me up. I'm Lilly, Gemma's grandmother. Kind of her to invite me. See, during the war I used to be–

**Mr Thomas**   Didn't know she was giving guided tours. Make sure you sterilize your shoes before you make contact with any of the cows. We don't want you bringing your Bryn Mawr germs up here.

**Gran**   If it's not convenient…

**Mr Thomas**   *[Sees Kate and Jane]* Here she is. *[As he walks past them]* If they get foot-an'-mouth, it'll be your fault.

*He goes.*

**Kate**   Lilly, I'd like you to meet Jane.

**Gran**   Hello my lovely.

*She strokes Jane's head.*

Oh Kate, I hope we haven't got you in trouble.

**Kate**   No, Lilly. We'll just make sure you've got proper footwear and clean hands, like I was going to do anyway. Jane's the best behaved of the herd. She'll let you milk her the old-fashioned way.

**Gemma**   *[To the audience]* Cowgirl had gone all chatty all of a sudden while she sorted everybody into wellies. Even Gran seemed at home.

**Kate**   Here you are, Lilly.

*Kate puts a stool down.*

**Gran**   It's been many years, Jane. I'll do my best.

*Gran begins to milk her.*

**Kate**  Natural, you are.

*Gran goes on until she's done.*

**Gran**  Ooh, I'd forgotten what a strain it was, bending over for long. Going to have a go, Gemma?

**Gemma**  Nah. Not bothered.

**Gran**  Oh, go on. It's not many times in life you get a chance to do something like this.

**Gemma**  No, thanks.

**Mr Banerjee**  I would like to try, please.

*The other cows gather around.*

**Kate**  Grandad told me we had over two hundred head of cattle before I was born. We had about fifty before the foot-and-mouth, and now twelve. These fields were all ours. Sold to Mostyn's farm now.

**Gran**  Old Miser Mostyn? But if they belong to him, how come you're still using it?

**Kate**  We rent it off him for the cows to graze. He wants it back.

**Gran**  You should bring them down to the common on the Mawr to graze for free. Your grandad used to. Kept the grass down lovely.

**Kate**  Can't. Dad says the cows will have to go to market.

**Gemma**  What does that mean?

**Kate**  Sold and killed probably.

**Mr Banerjee**  They've got lots to give yet.

**Gemma**  Aren't there any baby cows?

**Kate**  No They're away now.

**Gemma**  Why?

| | |
|---|---|
| **Gran** | Ever wondered how it is that cows give milk all year round? |
| **Gemma** | No. |
| **Gran** | Their calves are taken away from them and we take their milk because they carry on producing it. |
| **Gemma** | But the calves are their… babies! |
| **Kate** | But you want your milk from the supermarket like everyone else, don't you? |
| **Gemma** | What happens to them? |
| **Kate** | Eat them. |
| **Gemma** | I think I'm gonna be a vegetarian. |
| **Mr Banerjee** | In India we share the milk with the calves. |
| **Gran** | And you'd never kill the cow, isn't that right? |
| **Mr Banerjee** | Never. |
| | *Mr Thomas arrives.* |
| **Mr Thomas** | Kate, I think you've hit on a good sideline here. Farm tours with tea and cake thrown in. |
| **Gran** | I'd pay. You must be very proud of Kate. |
| **Mr Thomas** | Takes after her grandad. |
| **Gran** | I remember him well. He didn't say a lot but I liked him. And I've never seen anyone in my life work harder than your father. He was up before anyone else and in bed after everyone else. |
| **Mr Thomas** | He was a giant. |
| **Gran** | Kate's got his eyes. He wouldn't be happy about what's going on now. I'm sorry to hear things aren't so rosy for you these days. |
| **Mr Thomas** | *[To Kate]* Why don't you just phone the papers? |
| **Kate** | All I said was– |
| **Mr Thomas** | All you said was too much! |

| | |
|---|---|
| **Gran** | I didn't mean to cause offence, Mr Thomas. We should go. |
| **Mr Banerjee** | Right you are. |
| **Gran** | You're from a proud line, Kate. Don't forget it. I can't thank you enough, and you're always welcome to come for lunch at my home. |
| **Kate** | Thank you, Lilly. |
| **Gran** | [*To **Mr Thomas**]* I wish you and this farm well, whatever you choose to do. |

● ● ● ● ● ● ● ● ● ● ● ● ● ● ● ● ● ● ● ● ● ● ● ● ● ● ● ● ● ● ● ● ● ● ● ● ● ● ● ● ● ●

**SCENE 11**

| | |
|---|---|
| **Gemma** | [*To the audience]* I rode back down to Bryn Mawr and settled my gran back in. She didn't seem to want to talk. I've never known her so quiet. Then when I came out again… |
| | My bike! Where's my bike? |
| | *She looks.* |
| | Oi! You! My bike! Bring back my bike! |
| **Ryan** | [*With other kids]* Aw, what's the matter, Gemma? |
| **Gemma** | Who was it? Who took it? |
| **Ryan** | Took what? |
| **Gemma** | [*Grabs **Ryan**]* Who took it? |
| **Ryan** | When I tell Sian, you're dead. |
| **Gemma** | Who was it? |
| | *The kids go for her. **Karuna** turns up.* |
| **Karuna** | Hey! All you lot ganging up on one. |
| **Ryan** | What's it to you? |
| **Karuna** | Do your mothers know you do this? |
| **Ryan** | Jog on. |

26

*Karuna takes out a flute and brandishes it. The kids back off.*

| | |
|---|---|
| **Karuna** | Scared of music? |

*He plays the flute and advances on them. They run away.*

*[To Gemma]* What was all that about?

| | |
|---|---|
| **Gemma** | Someone stole my bike and they saw who it was. |
| **Karuna** | Your gran's my grandfather's neighbour, isn't she? |
| **Gemma** | Yeah. |
| **Karuna** | We should call the police. |
| **Gemma** | No point. It's gone now. |

*She bursts into tears and turns to go. Gran arrives.*

| | |
|---|---|
| **Gran** | Whatever's the matter, Gemma? |

*Gemma cries.*

| | |
|---|---|
| **Karuna** | Her bike got stolen. |
| **Gran** | Oh, Karuna. Was it locked? |
| **Karuna** | I think it was in your yard. |
| **Gemma** | I loved that bike. |
| **Gran** | Come here… |
| **Karuna** | I'd better go. |
| **Gemma** | *[Blurts]* I've always wanted to play the flute! |
| **Karuna** | Really? Come round some time and I'll give you a lesson. |
| **Gran** | Bye, Karuna. |

*Karuna leaves.*

| | |
|---|---|
| **Gemma** | *[Still crying]* Karuna? Karuna? |
| **Gran** | Yeah, Karuna. The flute?! |
| **Gemma** | Oh no. Why did he have to turn up just then? Look at me. The state of me. |

| Gran | Why didn't you lock your bike? |
| --- | --- |
| Gemma | Gran, don't you start! It got nicked, all right. My fault. I'm not blaming anyone except me, stupid me. |
| Gran | Where's my purse? |

*Gran* *digs out a £20 note.*

Here.

| Gemma | What's this? |
| --- | --- |
| Gran | Towards your new bike. Or you could always spend it on a flute. |

*Gemma* *smiles.*

That's better. I'll tell everybody to look out for your bike. You never know.

| Gemma | Thanks. See you, Gran. |
| --- | --- |

*Gran* *leaves.*

• • • • • • • • • • • • • • • • • • • • • • • • • • • • • • • • • • • • • •

## SCENE 12

*Gemma* *is on the way to school again.* *Sian* *is waiting.*

| Sian | Oi. You and me gonna talk. Why'd you hit Ryan? |
| --- | --- |
| Gemma | I didn't– |
| Sian | Liar. |
| Gemma | I didn't hit him. |
| Sian | Standing in the alley minding his own business, he was. Then you turn up and have a go. |

*Kate* *arrives.*

| Kate | Hello. |
| --- | --- |
| Sian | You keep out of this. *[To* *Gemma]* This your bodyguard? |

| Gemma | I didn't hit your brother. My bike got nicked and he saw who took it. |
|---|---|
| Sian | He said he didn't see nothing and you were asking him to grass. |
| Gemma | If he didn't see nothing he couldn't grass then, could he? |
| Sian | He says he didn't see who took it and I believe him. But I tell you what he did say – said your brother Darren was with them in the alley, and when you came out shouting, Ryan reckons your brother vanished. Maybe you should be looking closer to home before you go pointing fingers. We're not done, Cowgirl Two. Not by a long way. |

*She goes.*

| Kate | Your bike got nicked? |
|---|---|
| Gemma | Yeah. |
| Kate | Red, isn't it? |
| Gemma | It's a hybrid. |
| Kate | What's it called – the make, I mean? |
| Gemma | Vortex. |
| Kate | I'll keep an eye out for it. |

***Kate*** *leaves.*

• • • • • • • • • • • • • • • • • • • • • • • • • • • • • • • • • • • • • • • • • • • •

## SCENE 13

***Gemma*** *is in the supermarket with* ***Darren****.*

| Gemma | *[To the audience]* No bike meant walking to the shops on Saturday. And Mam made me take Darren. |
|---|---|
| | *[To* ***Darren****]* Get a move on, Darren. I don't wanna spend all my Saturday shopping. |
| Darren | Why didn't you just come on your own? |
| Gemma | Cos I lost my bike, didn't I? |

29

| Darren | Don't look at me. I didn't take your bike. |
| Gemma | You know who did. Sian told me. |
| Darren | Told you what? |
| Gemma | You were there. |
| Darren | Was not. I saw nothing! Telling Mam. |
| Gemma | You can tell Mam what you like but I know you were there and I won't forget, Darren. Your own sister's bike. Nasty, that is. |

*They see* **Morris**.

| Darren | God, he stinks. |
| Gemma | Not as bad as your story. Hello, Morris. |
| Morris | Go away. |
| Gemma | Sorry. |
| Morris | *[Holds out a tin of tomatoes]* Chopped or peeled? |
| Gemma | Chopped. |
| Morris | I need peeled tomatoes, not chopped. Cooking breakfast, I was. Emptied the can into the saucepan – they were chopped. Ruined that breakfast. |
| Gemma | Terrible. |
| Darren | Gemma! |
| Morris | Now, I need tinned corned beef. Tinned mind. |
| Darren | Gemma! |
| Gemma | Hold on, Darren. |
| Gemma | *[Locates the tins]* Here you are. Tinned corned beef. Two kinds. |
| Morris | Co-op own brand. |
| Gemma | Right. |

| | |
|---|---|
| **Morris** | Potato and leek soup – tin. |
| **Darren** | Morris, do yourself a favour – have a bath, man. |
| **Gemma** | *[To **Darren**]* Don't smell like a bunch of roses yourself! |
| **Darren** | All right! |
| | ***Gemma**'s phone beeps.* |
| **Gemma** | Anything else? |
| **Morris** | Carton of milk. Now. Go'way. |
| **Gemma** | *[Reading a text]* I don't believe it! Darren, come on. |
| **Darren** | What is it? |
| **Gemma** | Kate thinks she's found my bike. |
| **Darren** | Where? |
| **Gemma** | In the precinct. |
| **Darren** | Gran's shopping? |
| **Gemma** | Leave it. We'll get it later. |

● ● ● ● ● ● ● ● ● ● ● ● ● ● ● ● ● ● ● ● ● ● ● ● ● ● ● ● ● ● ● ● ● ● ● ● ● ● ● ● ● ● ● ● ● ● ● ● ● ●

## SCENE 14

*****Gemma** and **Darren** arrive where a man has the bike. **Kate** is next to him. **Gemma** looks at the bike.*

| | |
|---|---|
| **Gemma** | Yes! Yes! That's it! That's my bike! |
| **Bike man** | Well, anyone could come up and say that, couldn't they? |
| **Gemma** | Look. Scratches on the handlebars. The red mudguard. I put that on! |
| **Kate** | Where d'you buy it? |
| **Bike man** | A mate, all right? |
| **Kate** | Let's call the police. See what they say. |
| **Bike man** | Wait a minute. I paid money for this bike. Legit. |

| | |
|---|---|
| **Gemma** | It was stolen. |
| **Kate** | I think the police should be informed. |
| **Gemma** | Look. Here's twenty pounds. You can have that. |
| **Kate** | No, Gemma. It was stolen. He's giving it back because it's yours. Aren't you? |
| **Bike man** | *[Taking the note]* Reward money. Ta. |

***Bike man** is off.*

| | |
|---|---|
| **Kate** | Hey! |
| **Gemma** | Doesn't matter. I got it back. That was brilliant, Kate. |
| **Darren** | Lucky. |
| **Gemma** | Shut up, Darren. I still haven't forgiven you. Come and get the shopping. *[To **Kate**]* You coming round to Gran's? |
| **Kate** | Later. I got something to do. |
| **Gemma** | *[To the audience]* We found out what it was, Sunday. We went round Gran's for dinner. I went early on my bike. Mam and Darren walked. |

● ● ● ● ● ● ● ● ● ● ● ● ● ● ● ● ● ● ● ● ● ● ● ● ● ● ● ● ● ● ● ● ● ● ● ● ● ● ● ●

**SCENE 15**

*There is a crowd of neighbours round **Gran**'s yard.*

| | |
|---|---|
| **Gemma** | What's going on? Gran? Gran? What's going on? Are you all right? |

*The crowd part. **Jane** is standing there.*

| | |
|---|---|
| **Gran** | Look, Gemma. It's Jane. |
| **Gemma** | Jane? A cow? |
| **Gran** | You remember Jane. Isn't she beautiful? |
| **Gemma** | Course I remember her. What's she doing here? In your backyard? |
| **Gran** | Kate brought her down to see me. |

| | |
|---|---|
| **Kate** | Hiya. |
| **Gemma** | Oh, for the day, like? |
| **Gran** | No. Long as I like. Isn't that right? |
| **Kate** | She'll probably be better cared for here than up there. If she's too much trouble, I'll take her back. |
| **Roger** | It's bonkers. |
| **Gran** | Don't you start! It's my backyard. I'll do as I like. |
| **Roger** | What about the smell? The noise? |
| **Gran** | I have to put up with your smells and noises. |
| **Gemma** | What about food? |
| **Gran** | I'll go round and collect greenery for her. It'll keep me fit and I'll be doing this overgrown, shabby estate a favour. |
| **Mave** | Oh, Lilly, come on – a cow! |
| **Gran** | How many cats have you got? |
| **Mave** | Only two. What are you saying, Lil? Two cats are as much bother as a great hulking cow? |
| **Gran** | No, I'm not saying that, course not, but this beauty will give me milk to drink, and I can make butter and cheese as well. All she wants is grass and such. She'll earn her keep, not like the cats who just want a feed and a snooze. |
| | *Jane does a poo.* |
| **Gemma** | Oh no! Look now. |
| **Roger** | Great. It's going to stink to high heaven around here. |
| **Mr Banerjee** | I'll take it. Manure for my roses. They'll grow well. |
| **Gran** | There you are. Whenever Jane drops a load, I'll let you know, Mr Banerjee. You can count on it. |
| **Roger** | You won't have to tell him. He'll smell it. |
| | *Everyone starts to voice an opinion.* |

| Gran | I don't care. We've got plenty of real problems on the Bryn Mawr. This cow, Jane, she won't be smashing windows, or stealing, or shouting foul-mouthed abuse, or mugging you when you come back from the post office with your pension. No. She'll be good as gold, and give far more than she takes. And she'll be company. |
|---|---|
| Mr Banerjee | She'll bring us good luck. |

*Morris suddenly appears. Everyone goes quiet. Morris goes up to Jane and pats her.*

| Gran | Lovely isn't she, Morris? |
|---|---|
| Morris | I'll build her a shelter if you want, Lilly? |
| Gran | I think that's a cracking idea, Morris. |
| Morris | Got a tarpaulin in the attic. Won't be fancy but it'll do the job. |
| Roger | A tarpaulin? |
| Gran | A simple shelter is all she needs, Roger. Not the Great Wall of China. Thank you, Morris. Now, show's over. I want to settle her down for milking. Can I hear knocking at my front door? |
| Gemma | Aw heck. That'll be Mam. |
| Gran | Stay here. I'll let her in. |

*She goes.*

| Gemma | [To Kate] I just saw your dad. He said nothing about you bringing a cow down to Gran. |
|---|---|
| Kate | That's because he doesn't know. |

*Morris returns with the tarpaulin. The hanging of it begins.*

| Mam | [Enters] What the heck is going on here? A cow? Why couldn't you get a hamster like normal people? Ruby dying has turned your mind. [To Kate] You Kate? |
|---|---|
| Kate | Yeah. |

| | |
|---|---|
| **Mam** | Well, thank you, Kate. You can take it back now. |
| | *A **man with two children** turns up.* |
| **Man with children** | Excuse me? Could the kids have a look at the cow? Bit of a novelty, like. |
| **Gran** | Course they can. Bring them through. |
| **Mam** | Of all the stupid things I've seen in my life, Mam. Come on now, a great, lumping cow in your backyard. I mean, what for? |
| **Gran** | Milk, butter, cheese and company. |
| **Mam** | Company? Talking cow, is it? |
| **Gran** | No. And don't call her lumping – sensitive she is. Anyway, pot calling the kettle black. |
| **Mam** | It's a liability, Mam! |
| **Gran** | How? |
| **Mam** | How? It's a cow, that's how! |
| **Gran** | Ooh, that rhymes! *[Notices another family]* Oh hello, come to see Jane, have you? |
| **John** | If it's no trouble. I'm John, this is my wife, Mary, and these are the kids. We're from over the common. |
| **Gran** | No trouble, love. Follow me. |
| **John** | We're thinking of getting some chickens. |
| **Mam** | She's letting strangers through the house. |
| | ***Morris** appears.* |
| | And what's he doing? |
| **Morris** | I'm fixing up a shelter for Jane. |
| **Mam** | She's got a cow in the backyard, she's making cheese in a bucket, and a nutter roaming around. She's lost her ruddy marbles! |

*Mr Banerjee goes past with a bucket.*

| | |
|---|---|
| **John** | Ooh. Got any going spare? |
| **Mr Banerjee** | Yes, certainly. |
| **Gemma** | Hello, Mr Banerjee. |
| **Mr Banerjee** | Hello, Gemma. |

*Darren turns up with a load of grass and weeds.*

| | |
|---|---|
| **Darren** | These do, Gran? |
| **Gran** | That'll do lovely, Darren. |
| **Darren** | Can I feed her? |
| **Gran** | Aye, she likes fresh grass and such. |
| **Darren** | There's loads out back, Gran. I'll get some more. |
| **Gran** | Good boy, Darren! Good boy! |
| **Mam** | I don't believe it. |
| **Gemma** | Nor do I. |
| **Gran** | Due for a milking, aren't you, girl? Gemma, d'you fancy milking her? |
| **Gemma** | Yeah. Go on then. |

*She begins.*

| | |
|---|---|
| **Gran** | Pinch at the top, then squeeze with your hands. |
| **Gemma** | Like this? |
| **Gran** | Try again. Yeah, that's right. Lovely job. |

*Jamie and Ryan arrive.*

| | |
|---|---|
| **Roger** | Who said you could waltz in here, bold as brass? |
| **Ryan** | Come to see the cow, haven't we? |
| **Roger** | Right, well, there she is. Now hop it. |
| **Gran** | You can stay if you behave. |

| | |
|---|---|
| **Jamie** | Massive, innit? |
| **Darren** | Watch it! She's milking. Dangerous, she is now. Trample you to death if you're not careful. |
| **Ryan** | Crap. |
| **Jamie** | What's that coming out? |
| **Gran** | Milk, of course. Have your cornflakes dry, do you? |
| **Mr Banerjee** | Where did you think it came from then? |
| **Ryan** | Eeeeeew! |

*Jamie* and *Ryan* go.

| | |
|---|---|
| **Mam** | I'm worried, Mam, I got to say. |
| **Gran** | I can tell. Is it Robbie? |
| **Gemma** | Dad? Is he all right? |
| **Mam** | He's fine. I'm not worried about Robbie. It's you. |
| **Gran** | Me? |
| **Mam** | Yes, Mam. I know you must be sad losing Ruby, but a cow? |
| **Gran** | That cow has nothing to do with Ruby. Kate asked me if I fancied looking after her and I jumped at the chance. |
| **Mam** | And will this Kate give you money to look after her? |
| **Gran** | Now listen here. What I do in this house is my business, right? That cow won't cost me a penny. |
| **Darren** | *[Returning with more weeds]* Gran! This all right? Got it from Morris's garden. Said we were doing him a favour. |

*Jamie* and *Ryan* are *following him.*

| | |
|---|---|
| **Gran** | Spoil her, you will. Go on, be gentle. |

*The three boys feed* ***Jane***.

| | |
|---|---|
| | Don't go on, love. I'm having fun. I'll still help you out. |
| **Mam** | It's not that. I'm just worried about you. |

| Gran | You just concentrate on you and I'll look after me, right? |
| Mam | But how long are you going to keep it? |
| Gran | I'll keep *her* as long as Kate lets me. And by the way, your daughter has been a marvellous help. A star, she is. |
| Mam | Is she? |
| Darren | Mam! Mam! Jane ate tons of grass! |
| Gran | She's got four stomachs. |
| Darren | Four?! Wow, Jane. |
| Mam | It's a cow, Darren. It's not Jane. It's a cow. |
| Darren | People call their pets names, Mam, don't they? |
| Mam | It's not a pet. It's a cow! Haven't I got enough to worry about without my 80-year-old mam looking after a cow? |
| Darren | She's got plenty of help. We're all helping. |
| Mam | If you want to help, you can tidy your room. What about helping me, eh? Do your own washing and get the dinner underway. |
| Gemma | Sorry, Mam. |
| Darren | We can tell Dad about Jane tomorrow. |
| Gemma | I'd forgotten! |
| Mam | I'm sure he'll be fascinated. I don't know, a useless bloke in prison and a mam with a cow in her backyard. Happy days. |

• • • • • • • • • • • • • • • • • • • • • • • • • • • • • • • • • • • • • • • • • •

**SCENE 16**

*Gemma, Darren* and *Mam* are facing *Dad* at a table.

| Gemma | *[To the audience]* Visiting day. |
| Darren | You should see her, Dad. Massive she is. |
| Dad | What's this? |

| | |
|---|---|
| **Mam** | What he says – a cow at my mam's. |
| **Dad** | Joke, is it? |
| **Mam** | No. |
| **Dad** | Looking well, Claire. |
| **Mam** | Well, that'll be all the sun I'm getting. That and the restaurant food. |
| **Dad** | In the gym all the time now. And I'm up to a hundred press-ups. |
| **Darren** | She makes cheese and butter too. |
| **Dad** | Who does? |
| **Darren** | Gran, with the milk from Jane. |
| **Dad** | Who's Jane? |
| **Gemma** | The cow, Dad. We told you. All the neighbours are helping out, even Morris. |
| **Dad** | Oh. Sound. Hundred sit-ups too – rock hard, my stomach. You'll be well impressed, Claire. New man for you when I'm out. |
| **Mam** | Can't wait. What's his bank balance like? |
| **Dad** | Course I need loads of protein. So when I'm out I'll be eating this cow. |
| **Mam** | Your daughter's a veggie now. |
| **Dad** | What? Won't last long. |
| **Gemma** | I am, Dad. Don't want to eat animals any more. |
| **Dad** | You will if you're hungry enough. |
| **Gemma** | No, I won't. |
| **Dad** | I'll bet you a tenner you'll eat a burger by the time I get out. |
| **Mam** | Robbie, betting got you into enough trouble already, without you betting with your own daughter. |

| | |
|---|---|
| **Dad** | I'm only saying, love. I'm on your side. |
| **Mam** | There's no sides, Rob. When you get out you'll be back in the real world, and you'll have to earn your keep – a bit like Jane. |
| **Dad** | Who's Jane? |
| **Mam** | The COW! |

• • • • • • • • • • • • • • • • • • • • • • • • • • • • • • • • • • • • • • •

## SCENE 17

| | |
|---|---|
| | *Coming out of school.* **Gemma** *gets a call.* |
| **Gemma** | *[On the phone]* Kate? Where are you? |
| **Sian** | *[Catches up with* **Gemma***]* Oi. Where d'you think you're going? |
| **Gemma** | *[Ignores* **Sian** *and continues talking on the phone]* At Gran's? All right. All right. I'll see you there. *[Hangs up]* |
| **Sian** | Ignoring me? |
| **Gemma** | I've just got to go to my gran's. |
| **Sian** | Cowgirl's learning you fast, isn't she? |
| **Gemma** | Cows get a rotten life, you know. Well, I mean, all they do is eat grass, and when they have a calf it's taken away as soon as it's born, so's we can take their milk. |
| **Sian** | So? |
| **Gemma** | That's a rotten life, don't you reckon? |
| **Sian** | Not bothered. |
| **Gemma** | No. I suppose not. Not many are. |
| **Sian** | You trying to be funny? |
| **Gemma** | No. Are you? |
| | **Gemma** *steps forward.* **Sian** *backs off.* **Gemma** *laughs.* **Sian** *grabs her. A fight begins. A* **teacher** *arrives and separates them.* |

40

It's a misunderstanding, Sir. I was just telling Sian what a rotten life cows have, what with being killed so young just for burgers and such. She thought I was talking about her, but I wasn't. I was talking about cows. They give us their milk and all the thanks they get is being slaughtered before they even get into Year 1!

Bye, Sian. Moo.

• • • • • • • • • • • • • • • • • • • • • • • • • • • • • • • • • • • • • • • • • • • • • • • • • •

## SCENE 18

*At **Gran's**. **Kate** is there.*

| | |
|---|---|
| **Kate** | What happened to your eye? |
| **Gemma** | Doesn't matter. What's going on here? |

*A large group of old people are sitting around.*

| | |
|---|---|
| **Gran** | Sit down, Gemma. We've talking to do. |
| **Kate** | We've been waiting for you. |
| **Gran** | Fancy some cheese, courtesy of Jane? |
| **Gemma** | Are we having a cheese tasting? |
| **Gran** | No, we're not. Kate's dad knows a cow is missing. |
| **Kate** | I told him. |
| **Gemma** | What happened? |
| **Kate** | He blew his top. Got straight on the phone to Don Mostyn and cut a deal. He'll be coming to collect them any day. |
| **Gemma** | Gran, why don't you buy, Jane? |
| **Gran** | Thought of that, love. Well over a grand, a good cow like Jane is worth. I haven't got that kind of money. Wish I had. |
| **Gemma** | What'll Mostyn do with them? |
| **Kate** | He'll take them straight into his herd, calve them once or twice maybe, and then straight to slaughter. He just wants his field back and the money he's owed. |

41

| | |
|---|---|
| **Roger** | The miser. |
| **Gran** | I love having that cow here. |
| **Roger** | Lovely cheese she makes. |
| **Mr Banerjee** | She brings us peace. |
| **Morris** | Aye. |
| **Mave** | The cream I made from that milk was like nothing I've ever tasted. |
| **Gemma** | So, what's happening? |
| **Gran** | Well, they don't know where Jane is as yet, so we decided, or Kate has suggested, that we take the rest. |

*Around this point, the old people begin to transform into cows.*

| | |
|---|---|
| **Gemma** | How do you mean 'the rest'? |
| **Gran** | We want the whole dozen down here, on the estate. It's all hush-hush though. |
| **Gemma** | You want to bring eleven cows down here. On to the Bryn Mawr? |
| **Gran** | That's right. |
| **Kate** | Yeah. |
| **Gemma** | You're mad, you are. Absolutely mad! |

*Gemma, Kate and Gran are now standing at the head of a jostling herd of cows.*

*Interval.*

# ACT TWO

**SCENE 1**

> *The cast assembled as cattle.* **Gemma** *and* **Kate** *are with them.*
> **Darren** *arrives.*

| | |
|---|---|
| **Darren** | Gemma! Gemma! |
| **Gemma** | Go home, Darren. |
| **Darren** | I wanna come. I want to help you with the cows. |
| **Gemma** | Darren, you got to be in school. |
| **Darren** | But you won't be, why can't I? |
| **Gemma** | Because if I don't show we'll get away with it, but not both of us. |
| **Kate** | Gemma. |
| **Gemma** | What? |
| **Kate** | We could use the help. |
| **Gemma** | *[To **Darren**]* If you mess up this mission… |
| **Darren** | I won't. |
| **Gemma** | If you mess this up, Gran will lose Jane. |
| **Darren** | I won't… I won't… |

> **Jamie** *turns up.*

| | |
|---|---|
| **Gemma** | What's he doing here? |
| **Darren** | Coming with us? |
| **Gemma** | What? You told him? |
| **Darren** | He'll help, Gemma. |
| **Kate** | We'd better get going. |
| **Gemma** | All right, then. You can both help. |

SCENE 1

ACT TWO

| Jamie | Lush. |
| Gemma | If you can keep up. |
| Kate | Ready? |
| Gemma | Quiet, isn't it? |
| Kate | They been milked and fed. I'll lead them, you follow at the back. |
| Gemma | What do we have to do? |
| Kate | Nothing, just keep them from stopping. |
| Darren | What if they turn around? |
| Kate | They won't. They might get distracted by grass at the side of the lane, but they'll follow the others. When I hold them up at the front, they'll all stop. When you see us moving off, just clap your hands and shout 'Get along!' and they'll move. |
| Jamie | What if they don't? |
| Gemma | Shut up, Jamie. |
| Kate | OK. Let's go. Go on! GO ON! |
| Jamie | What? Go where? |
| Kate | NOT YOU! The cows. |
| Gemma | Go on. |
| Darren | Get along. |
| Jamie | Go on then. |

*One of the cows looks at them and moos.*

That's cow language for 'Who are you to tell me what to do?'

| Darren | She won't move. |
| Kate | That's Rachel. Stubborn, she is. Shout at her like you shout at your brother. |
| Gemma | Rachel! Get along! |

| | |
|---|---|
| **Darren** | That's not how you talk to me. |
| **Gemma** | GET ALONG! GET! |
| **Kate** | That's the way. Come on girls. |
| **Darren** | Wagons roll! |
| **Jamie** | Go on! |

● ● ● ● ● ● ● ● ● ● ● ● ● ● ● ● ● ● ● ● ● ● ● ● ● ● ● ● ● ● ● ● ● ● ● ●

**SCENE 2**

| | |
|---|---|
| **Gemma** | *[To the audience]* And we were off! We set off down the lane. Oh my God! |
| **Kate** | We're coming up to a crossroads. Keep 'em moving. |
| | ***Mr Jarvis*** *pulls up in a car.* |
| **Mr Jarvis** | Where you off with them, Kate? |
| **Kate** | Bit of exercise, Mr Jarvis. |
| **Mr Jarvis** | Shouldn't you be at school? |
| **Kate** | Bring and tell. |
| **Mr Jarvis** | *[To **Gemma**]* Is she really taking them into school? |
| **Gemma** | That's right. Not into the classroom though. That would be ridiculous, wouldn't it? |
| **Mr Jarvis** | Bye then. |
| **Kate** | See you. |
| | ***Mr Jarvis*** *drives off. They pause.* |
| | All right? |
| **Jamie** | Yeah. |
| **Darren** | Brilliant. |
| **Gemma** | Going OK, isn't it? |
| **Kate** | Yeah. |

| Jamie | I got some chocolate. |
| Darren | Share it, Jamie. |
| Jamie | What, do cows eat chocolate? |
| Gemma | No, with us, you daft– |
| Jamie | All right. |
| Gemma | Chocolate always tastes better when you've saved it up. |
| Kate | *[About the cows]* They're enjoying themselves. |
| Gemma | Which one's that? |
| Kate | Donna. Bit slow is Donna – she's easily scared. I'm putting her with Morris. |
| Gemma | Aw. That's nice. |

*A car horn sounds.*

| Kate | If that's Dad, it's over. |

***Mrs Conway** pulls up.*

| Mrs Conway | Kate, what's going on here? |
| Kate | They got out, Mrs Conway. Boys from the Mawr, we reckon. If you back up I'll get them past you. |
| Mrs Conway | But you need to go that way, don't you? |
| Kate | There's no passing bay. You back up and we'll get them past you. |
| Mrs Conway | There's kind of you, girl. |

*She goes.*

| Kate | Close one. Get 'em moving. |

*They wave, smiling.*

We've got eleven cows to take into the Bryn Mawr. There's a field just over the bridge. Once we get them over that, they can graze there and then we'll take a few at a time on to the Bryn Mawr.

## SCENE 3

**Gemma**   *[To the audience]* We took the cows over the motorway bridge. Down below the cars were zooming by. Swansea the one way, London the other. And there we were, high above them with the cows, as if they were saying 'What's the rush?' I hadn't realised I'd been holding my breath until we got to the other side. *[She breathes out]* That's a relief!

**Kate**   Right. One of you needs to stay here – I don't want them injuring themselves on any sharp objects. Darren, you stay. You get to watch over six cows. Reckon you can do it?

**Darren**   Yeah.

**Kate**   Right. We'll take Rachel, Connie, Megan, Suzie and Bess first.

**Gemma**   Right.

**Kate**   Be firm with them. Check around for metal and stuff they might hurt themselves on.

**Darren**   Right.

**Kate**   OK?

**Darren**   Yeah. Come on girls. Let's just hope we don't meet Mam.

*__Darren__ leaves with his six cows. __Jamie__ follows.*

## SCENE 4

**Gemma**   *[To the audience]* So, down the hill, across a crossing. *[Beeping]* We were past the busiest part of the route and now we were on the Mawr Estate. The first drop-off was Megan to Mr Llewellyn.

*The cows change into the humans who are going to take them.*

**Mr Llewellyn**   Welcome, Megan. I've built a pen for her – a cow sty, I suppose you could say.

| | |
|---|---|
| **Kate** | Plenty of hay. That's good. She won't need milking again until this evening. Any problems, call Lilly and she'll get hold of me. |
| **Mr Llewellyn** | Right you are. |
| **Gemma** | *[As they move on]* He'd better look after her. Mr and Mrs Evans were next. *[To **Mr** and **Mrs Evans**]* Here you go. See you, Bess. |
| **Mrs Evans** | Hello, Bess love. |
| **Mr Evans** | This is madness! |
| **Mrs Evans** | *[To **Gemma**]* Pay no heed. |
| **Mr Evans** | But it's not legal, is it? |
| **Kate** | They're my cows. I'm giving them to you, temporary like. If there's a problem… |
| **Mrs Evans** | Oh no, there's no problem, love. You agreed, Ron. I want this cow and she's staying. I put up with your smoking, your beer and your betting. You're going to accept this cow, or you can cook and clean for yourself. Understood? |
| **Mr Evans** | Yes, dear. |
| **Gemma** | *[As they move on, to the audience]* Well told off, he was. The others were all straightforward. Maria Bracchi, who used to own the Italian on the High Street. Mrs Oleski… |
| **Kate** | She bakes her own bread. |
| **Gemma** | *[To the audience]* And the Choudarys. Their kids were in our school. Then back up the hill to Darren. |

• • • • • • • • • • • • • • • • • • • • • • • • • • • • • • • • • • • • • • • • • • • •

**SCENE 5**

*Back with **Darren**, **Jamie** and the six cows.*

| | |
|---|---|
| **Kate** | Well done, Darren, now you two get off to school. |
| **Jamie** | What? |

| | |
|---|---|
| **Kate** | Too many of us out. Go back. We can manage this lot. They're for the terrace. |
| | *The boys go.* **Kate** *sighs.* |
| **Gemma** | What's wrong? It's going well. |
| **Kate** | 'Cept it's hardly a secret, is it? |
| **Gemma** | Word gets around. |
| **Kate** | That Mr Evans was right. It is a mad idea. |
| **Gemma** | But we'll be saving them from slaughter. You said yourself that they've got years of life left in them. And if it wasn't for Mostyn… |
| | **Kate** *doesn't reply.* |
| **Gemma** | Which one's that one? |
| **Kate** | Rhiannon. |
| **Gemma** | Who's she going to? |
| **Kate** | Roger. |
| **Gemma** | Bad luck, Rhiannon. |
| **Kate** | Dad's going to be fuming. |
| **Gemma** | But he says the cows don't earn you any money. |
| **Kate** | Doesn't mean to say he won't be fuming when he finds out they're all gone. And it's not going to take long for him to hear where they are. |
| **Gemma** | We can keep a secret on the Mawr if we need to. What about your grandad? What do you think he would've done? |
| **Kate** | Maybe he would have carried on and it would have been all right. Maybe he would have made it worse. He couldn't have stopped the foot-and-mouth outbreak. I remember Grandad talking about it. I was a baby then. Farmers didn't just lose the cows, they lost all the milk those cows would have given if they'd lived – thousands of litres. So when the second outbreak came, after he died, I knew what it would mean for |

us. It wasn't Dad's fault, but I was angry because I thought he didn't care.

**Gemma**     Didn't care about the cows being killed, you mean?

**Kate**      They sent me away, while it was sorted. I lost it big time... I didn't want to go to my aunt's in Monmouth. It felt like I was leaving the cows when they needed me. I remember Dad had to hold me while he tried to open the truck. You still see the dent where I kicked the door... When they brought me back to the farm, the cows were gone. There was a massive circle of black on the ground where they'd been burned. I could smell it in the air. Dad said it was my imagination, but it wasn't. It was there, a horrible stink that didn't go away. There's times I can still smell it.

He tries hard, my dad.

**Gemma**     My dad's in prison. He used to take us out on trips. Well, he did once. He took us to that waterfall. Do you know it?

**Kate**      Waterfall?

**Gemma**     Yeah. It's around here someplace, and there's a field with a big tree. I want to find it. But I don't know how.

**Kate**      Ordnance Survey?

**Gemma**     What's that?

**Kate**      It's a map.

**Gemma**     But I don't know where the place is.

**Kate**      You said there was a stream and a waterfall, not far from here.

**Gemma**     Yeah.

**Kate**      Well, everything like hills and streams will all be marked on the Ordnance Survey maps – process of elimination.

**Gemma**     But where can I get them?

**Kate**      We got some.

| Gemma | Will you… Will you help me? |
| Kate | OK. |
| Gemma | Thanks. |
| Kate | Is your dad in prison long? |
| Gemma | He'll be out next month. Stupid. My brother thinks he's great. Hero in his eyes. Stupid boys. |
| Kate | Yeah, bulls are nowhere near as nice as cows, or as useful. Bullocks are thick and bulls are dangerous and unpredictable. |
| Gemma | What's the difference between bullocks and bulls? |
| Kate | Bullocks have had their bits cut off. |
| Gemma | Ugh! Why? |
| Kate | So they're easier to manage. Then they're just fed for meat – slaughtered after a couple of years. |
| Gemma | Wait till I tell Darren. |
| Kate | I think we should take them back. |
| Gemma | Bit early. |
| Kate | No. I mean back up to the farm. |
| Gemma | What? |

• • • • • • • • • • • • • • • • • • • • • • • • • • • • • • • • • • • •

## SCENE 6

*Darren rushes on.*

| Darren | Gemma! |
| Gemma | What, Darren? |

*A load of children emerge, led by **Jamie**.*

| Darren | Look! |
| Gemma | Jamie, what d'you bring them for? |

| Jamie | They wanna help. |
| Gemma | The whole thing'll be ruined. |
| Jamie | They all knew anyway. That's Johnny Bracchi – his gran's got one of the cows. And that's Chloe Llewellyn. |
| Darren | I took one down this morning. On a lead, like a massive dog. |
| Gemma | Do you still want to take them back up to the farm? |
| Cow | NOOOOOO! |
| Kate | OK. We haven't got much time. You can help take 'em down. But don't make any sudden moves, and as soon as we get 'em to their owners you all go back to school like nothing happened. If anyone asks, you don't know anything. The cows are coming home. |

*They set out. A **policeman** arrives.*

| Policeman | Where you lot off to with them? |
| Kate | Taking them on to the Mawr Common for a school project. Questions and answers. |
| Policeman | Lot of work for a school project, isn't it? And six cows? |
| Kate | Two classes. See, one cow might get nervous with loads of kids around it. |
| Policeman | When I was at school we had to make do with a guinea pig. Aren't you supposed to inform Defra if you move cows? |
| Kate | Only if it's permanent. We'll be taking them back up directly. |
| Darren | Four stomachs a cow has. Put grass in one end and you get milk out the other – milk for your cornflakes. |
| Policeman | That's put me off my breakfast. Get along then. I don't want to hear about any cows on the rampage later. OK? |
| Darren | Yes, Sir. |
| Kate | *[As the **policeman** goes]* That was a tight one. |

## SCENE 7

| | |
|---|---|
| **Gemma** | *[To the audience]* So, long story short, we got them all to their new homes. |
| | ***Morris** enters.* |
| **Morris** | Hello, girl. |
| **Gemma** | *[To the audience]* Morris was last. |
| | *[To **Morris**]* Morris. This is Donna. |
| **Morris** | She's nervous. Like me. |
| **Gemma** | They all are, Morris. |
| **Morris** | Got grass and wild flowers for her. |
| **Gemma** | You had a bath, Morris! |
| **Morris** | Special occasion, see. Come on, girl. |
| **Gemma** | And that was the lot. |

• • • • • • • • • • • • • • • • • • • • • • • • • • • • • • • • • • • • • • • • • • • • • • • • • • • •

## SCENE 8

*Home.* ***Gemma**, **Mam** and **Darren** are there.*

| | |
|---|---|
| **Mam** | Good day at school, was it? |
| **Gemma** | Not bad. |
| **Mam** | Funny. Cos the school phoned me asking where you both were. 'Should be there,' I said. 'Well they're not,' they said. I remembered how quiet you both were this morning. Should I call the police? I thought. But then Billy Jones came in for the late shift at work and says, 'Just saw your Gemma taking some cows across the high street.' Not one cow, but cows. Plural. So I headed to the Mawr in my break and I spotted you with that Kate girl, and three cows. Little Jamie Thorpe was with you too, so I figured Darren was on duty elsewhere. |

That's right, your mam's a reg'lar Miss Marple. Now tell me, did you really think you could take a load of cows through town without me knowing about it? Because if you did you must be as stupid as you think I am!

I said I didn't want your gran getting another pet, you remember? Then the cow turns up and I tell her that I'm not happy, what with the strain and the extra costs and suchlike. But everyone tells me it's fine cos it's a cow and they're useful. Then the next thing you help take another eleven down here. ELEVEN!

**Gemma**  But they're not all at Gran's, Mam.

**Mam**  That's beside the point. And you, Darren! Gone all cosy with your sister now, haven't you?

**Darren**  How d'you mean 'cosy'?

**Gemma**  Mam, it's not like we brought one here, is it? They're with other people.

**Mam**  But you didn't tell me, did you? 'Oh Mam, d'you mind if I help take some cows down on to the Mawr Estate tomorrow?' No. You did it behind my back. How d'you think that makes me feel? My mam and my own daughter in cahoots!

**Darren**  What's 'cahoots'?

**Mam**  And the sheer stupidity of it! How long do you think you can keep eleven cows hushed up?

**Darren**  Twelve.

**Gemma**  But they'll be slaughtered.

**Mam**  Oh really? And how many cows do you think have been killed since you two were born?

**Gemma**  Loads.

**Mam**  Loads. Right, and so what makes these ones so special?

**Darren**  Mam, they're great. Don't diss 'em. They're massive, useful and good, they are.

| | |
|---|---|
| **Mam** | I don't care about cows, Darren. I care about making ends meet, paying bills, getting the food in to feed us, making sure you've got clothes and… and Robbie's back soon… The useless… Fed up, I am. |
| **Gemma** | Sorry, Mam, we didn't do it behind your back on purpose. We just didn't think. |
| **Mam** | D'you realize I'm in every night? Three hundred and sixty-five days a year. Every night! You read in the papers about women that leave their young children home alone… I know why they do it. But I haven't, and I wouldn't. |
| **Gemma** | But Mam, we could go to Gran's if you fancied a bingo night. |
| **Mam** | Yeah, 'specially now you've got the cow to visit. That cow gets more… |
| **Darren** | Mam, are you jealous of Jane? |
| **Mam** | Tomorrow you're both in school all day. Understood? |
| **Gemma** | Yes, Mam. |
| **Mam** | Promise me now. |
| **Gemma and Darren** | We promise, Mam. |
| **Mam** | And any bright ideas you get, like opening a zoo, you ask me first. Right? |
| **Gemma and Darren** | Right. |
| **Darren** | Mam, if there was a spare cow going…? |
| **Mam** | NO! |
| **Gemma** | *[To the audience]* Course, everyone knew about the cows. |
| **Girl** | Hiya, Gemma. Going round to Mrs Oleski's later to see Rachel. |
| **Gemma** | Oh yeah? |

| Boy | Gemma, my dad wants to know if there's any chance of a cow? |
| --- | --- |
| Gemma | Not at the moment, no. |
| | *[To the audience]* They never usually even talk to me! I got to go to Morris's. |

● ● ● ● ● ● ● ● ● ● ● ● ● ● ● ● ● ● ● ● ● ● ● ● ● ● ● ● ● ● ● ● ● ● ● ● ● ● ● ● ●

**SCENE 9**

*At **Morris**'s house.*

| Morris | Go away! I'm feeding Donna. |
| --- | --- |
| Girl | We just wanna look. |
| Morris | Looking's no good. Get her some food. One at a time, please. I don't want her frightened. |
| Boy | How much she weigh, d'you reckon? |
| Gran | *[Arriving]* Enough to break your toe if she trod on your foot. |
| Boy | She's not stopped eating. |
| Morris | Well, she's got a lot of stomachs to fill. |
| Darren | *[Arriving]* Four! Look, Morris, fresh grass off the school caretaker. Plenty more where that came from. |
| Gran | Kate came by. |
| Gemma | How was she? |
| Gran | Oh, she looked as white as snow, Gemma. She's fighting her dad, and I'm worried we played the wrong hand. I mean, a dozen cows and on the Bryn Mawr of all places! |
| Gemma | Well, they're here now, Gran, and look, everyone's into it and they'll be well cared for. Just think of them sliced up in the butcher's after Mostyn's done with them. |
| Gran | Oh, Gemma! |
| Gemma | Well, it's true, Gran. I'll go up to the farm to see her. |

| | |
|---|---|
| **Gran** | Good idea. Oh, she left a map for you. Here. |
| | *She gives **Gemma** a map. **Gemma** opens it up.* |
| | She's circled places. What's it for? |
| **Gemma** | Nothing important. School. |
| **Gran** | Darren told me about your mam. I'll call her later, tell her you're on an errand from me and I'll invite her for dinner. We'll make peace. |
| | *__Mr Banerjee__ arrives. He begins to put flowers in **Donna's** hair.* |
| **Mr Banerjee** | Hello Lilly, come around. We are celebrating. |
| **Gemma** | Hello Mr Banerjee. How's Karuna? |
| **Mr Banerjee** | Karuna is not here. How's your flute playing? |
| **Gemma** | Not much good. It's hard. |
| **Mr Banerjee** | But if you keep practising you'll soon have birds coming to your window to listen. |
| **Gemma** | How's Peggy doing? |
| **Mr Banerjee** | Fine. She has a good heart and gives me much milk because she is free, like in India. |
| **Gemma** | I'm on my way to find Kate. I'll tell her. |

● ● ● ● ● ● ● ● ● ● ● ● ● ● ● ● ● ● ● ● ● ● ● ● ● ● ● ● ● ● ● ● ● ● ● ● ● ● ● ●

## SCENE 10

| | |
|---|---|
| | *The farm.* |
| **Gemma** | *[To the audience]* I went up the farm and found Kate sitting in the road. |
| | You all right? |
| **Kate** | Dad's called Defra. |
| **Gemma** | Who's Defra? |
| **Kate** | The government department that deals with farming and stuff. You have to tell them when cows are moved, by law. Stupid. |

| | |
|---|---|
| **Gemma** | Who? Your dad? |
| **Kate** | No! Me! Me! This whole thing was stupid. Taking the cows to the Mawr sorted nothing out. Nothing. They don't have farms in the middle of towns. |
| **Gemma** | They do! In cities even! Maybe we could have one of those! |
| **Kate** | There's no time for that. My dad's fuming. He'd already gone and put a deposit down on that tree shredder he was talking about. |
| **Gemma** | So? |
| **Kate** | Think about it! Mostyn's got his field back, but my dad still owes him. All he had to pay him with was the cows – the cows we've got. Dad can't believe I did it, and nor can I. |
| **Gemma** | Oh no. Don't cry. You're the cowgirl. The cowgirl. You don't cry. |
| **Mr Thomas** | *[Arriving]* Good fun, is it? Where are they? What's the point? What are you going to solve doing this? When I told Mostyn I had no cows to sell him, he thought I was having a laugh. And the chap from Defra told me to call the police, so I said, 'Well, they haven't exactly been stolen.' 'How d'you mean?' he says. 'Kate, my daughter, took them.' 'Where to?' he asks. 'I don't know,' I says. 'This is very irregular,' he tells me. Irregular! What you've done is completely insane! |
| **Kate** | You didn't try, Dad. I understood when the cows were taken to slaughter. I felt sad, but I knew it was the way. Then foot-and-mouth came – the plague, you called it – but it was like you caught it instead of the cows. You gave in to Mostyn… |
| **Mr Thomas** | Gave in! Those cows are a liability – it's nothing to do with Mostyn. |
| **Kate** | You stopped being a farmer, Dad, but I didn't, and I still haven't. Grandad saw this coming. |
| **Mr Thomas** | When he was alive, the herd was already running at a loss. That's what you don't see. |

| Kate | I don't mean that. I mean you! One day he was in the milking shed talking to Grandma about you – they didn't know I was there. He said you didn't have the stomach for farming. He called it right, didn't he? You never had the stomach for it. But it's not the cows' fault, is it? They've done nothing wrong. Nothing! |
|---|---|

*She goes.*

| **Mr Thomas** | Where are the cows? |
|---|---|
| **Gemma** | What cows? |

• • • • • • • • • • • • • • • • • • • • • • • • • • • • • • • • • • • • • • • • • • • •

## SCENE 11

| **Gemma** | *[To the audience]* I got on my bike and pedalled. If ever I needed a waterfall to wash it all away, it was now. The last of the three circles Kate had drawn was the furthest from the Bryn Mawr. 'Maes-glas Forest'. It was a bit spooky. |
|---|---|

*Gemma leaves the bike. Checks her phone.*

No signal?

Nothing seems familiar. This can't be it.

*A gust of wind.*

I'd best go back.

And then I heard it. Water.

There has to be a stream nearby.

*Gemma pushes forward. Then sees it.*

That's it! The waterfall! The one Dad and Darren had stuck their heads under. That's it. It seems smaller somehow. And different.

*She looks around.*

We must have been here in the summer.

*She puts her hand in the water.*

Ice cold. Tumbling and sloshing, going on forever. All that water. All that rain. Never stops raining in Wales. Mam! Dad!

I shouldn't have come. You can't go back. You shouldn't even try. It's all small and overgrown and different.

*She empties her box of leaves.*

Here you are. Take it back. I've come all the way here, but it isn't the same. Why did I think it would be?

• • • • • • • • • • • • • • • • • • • • • • • • • • • • • • • • • • • • • • • • • • • •

## SCENE 12

|  |  |
|---|---|
|  | *She heads to **Gran**'s.* |
| **Gemma** | *[To the audience]* I got on my bike and cycled back to Gran's. |
|  | *She sees **Karuna** on the ground. He is injured.* |
|  | Karuna! You all right? What happened? |
| **Karuna** | They didn't get my flute. |
| **Mam** | *[Arriving]* Gemma? |
| **Gemma** | Mam! It's Karuna. He's been beaten up. |
| **Mam** | Come on, son. Can you walk? We should call the police. |
| **Mr Banerjee** | *[Arriving]* No. I'll call his father and mother first. |
| **Mam** | Well, let's clean him up. I wouldn't like to see my boy in this state. |
| **Karuna** | Ow! |
| **Mam** | No broken bones. |
| **Gemma** | Who was it, Karuna? |
| **Karuna** | No idea. They came from behind and grabbed my flute. |
| **Mr Banerjee** | Why do people do this? We are a peace-loving family and would not harm the smallest creature. |

| | |
|---|---|
| **Mam** | This is not the sort of welcome we want the Bryn Mawr giving newcomers. There is no reason for it. It makes me ashamed. |
| **Gemma** | We can stop it! I'm fed up of it, Mam. We can stop it if we want. |
| **Mam** | I'm fed up of it too. It's not everyone, just a few that don't understand what they do, or even why they do it. |
| **Mr Banerjee** | Your daughter is right. We can stop it, if we want. |
| | ***Karuna*** plays his flute. |
| **Karuna** | Sounds OK. We could have that lesson tomorrow. |
| | ***Mr Banerjee*** and ***Karuna*** leave. |
| **Mam** | The flute? |
| **Gemma** | I thought you'd laugh. |
| **Mam** | Who's laughing? Very nice of him. |
| | ***Mam*** goes. |
| **Darren** | *[Arriving]* Who d'you reckon beat up him next door then? |
| **Gemma** | Him next door?! He's got a name. You think it's funny, Darren? |
| **Darren** | Sorry. Gary Tobin nicked your bike. |
| **Gemma** | What? |
| **Darren** | I didn't know he was going to do it, Gemma, honest. |
| **Gemma** | S'all right. Got it back now. |
| **Darren** | I got scared of what he might do if I grassed on him – nasty, he is. He doesn't like the cows either. |
| **Gemma** | He's like Sian. Can't stand people mingling together. They need it to be 'them' and 'us'. They're always fighting. They depend on it. I don't want to feel that any more. |

## SCENE 13

*At the Banerjees. **Gemma** is with **Karuna**.*

**Karuna**  First lesson. Take this bottle. And blow across the top.

**Gemma**  Why?

**Karuna**  Who's the teacher?

***Gemma** does it and gets a sound.*

**Gemma**  Oh my God!

All these figures around your house. Who are they?

**Karuna**  They're all Hindu gods and goddesses.

**Gemma**  Who's that?

**Karuna**  That's Durga. She slays demons. Ten arms and rides a lion.

**Gemma**  Useful or what?

**Karuna**  That's Krishna.

**Gemma**  He's blue!

**Karuna**  He's a god and a cowherd.

**Gemma**  We've only got Tom Jones in our house. And he's broken.

*She blows again.*

Play me something. Anything.

**Karuna**  All right. This is Bach.

*He plays. **Gemma** is visibly moved.*

**Gemma**  I got to go.

**Karuna**  Are you all right?

**Gemma**  Thank you. That was… That was beautiful.

*She leaves **Karuna**.*

**SCENE 14**

| | |
|---|---|
| **Gemma** | *[To the audience]* I felt good, like everything was going to be all right. Then Morris went and took Donna for a walk on the Common. |
| | ***Morris*** *has* ***Donna*** *on a tether. He has a crowd around him.* |
| **Gemma** | Morris! Morris! What are you doing out here on the Common? |
| **Morris** | She needed a walk. |
| **Gemma** | But out here? Anyone could see her. |
| **Morris** | Getting frustrated she was. Loads of fresh grass here doing nothing. |
| **Woman** | Is this one of the Bryn Mawr dozen? |
| **Morris** | Aye, that's right. |
| | *Others arrive.* |
| **Roger** | Bloody Morris. I'm going to give you a piece of my mind. |
| **Gran** | You'll do no such thing! He was thinking about Donna. |
| **Morris** | It's done her a power of good. Maybe she misses being with the others too, don't you think? |
| **Gran** | Perhaps he's right. Kate, you say the word and they can all go back up to that field of theirs. |
| **Mave** | Oh Lil, no! My Maisy's settled in lovely now. |
| **Gran** | They're not ours to decide. Those cows belong to Kate and Mr Thomas, and if the best thing is to take them back, then that's what we'll do. |
| **Darren** | No, Gran! Don't give 'em back, please. They'll be killed. |
| **Gran** | Shush now, Darren. I've been pleased as punch the way you've taken to that cow – you've been a different boy – but this can't go on forever. |

| | |
|---|---|
| **Gemma** | But they'll be killed. |
| **Gran** | Shall I have a word with your father, Kate? |
| **Kate** | He's too angry. He's not even talking to me at the moment. Besides the cows are here now. We won't do them any favours moving them again. |
| **Gran** | But they're still yours, Kate. We haven't forgotten that. |

*Everyone goes, leaving **Gemma** and **Kate**.*

| | |
|---|---|
| **Gemma** | You want to borrow my bike? |
| **Kate** | No. |
| **Gemma** | It'll take you ages to get home. |
| **Kate** | No! |

***Kate** goes.*

• • • • • • • • • • • • • • • • • • • • • • • • • • • • • • • • • • • • • • • • • • • • •

## SCENE 15

*The prison waiting room. **Mam**, **Gemma** and **Darren**.*

| | |
|---|---|
| **Gemma** | *[To the audience]* The next time we went to visit Dad. |
| **Mam** | Listen to this, Robbie. *[Reads from the newspaper]* 'The cows have made a big difference to the estate since they arrived, an anonymous caller claimed. And people love them. No one would say where the cows are, but Local Councillor Rhys Morgan admitted, "Things are strangely quiet on the Bryn Mawr. The police informed me that domestic incidents are down and we've had no burglaries in a while. I've not seen any cows, mind you, though I have heard the odd moo late at night."' |
| **Dad** | Who d'you reckon called them? |
| **Mam** | Dunno. My mam reckons it was Roger but he swears blind he didn't. |
| **Dad** | The Mawr never ceases to amaze me. Your mam ought to sell her cow while she's got the chance. |

| | |
|---|---|
| **Gemma** | How d'you mean? |
| **Dad** | Well, I bet she could find someone to take it off her hands. |
| **Darren** | No, Dad. Fantastic, it is. |
| **Mam** | I don't think she'd sell it for a million, Rob. She's really taken to it, and her neighbours – some of them have got one an' all. |
| **Dad** | Oh aye. *[To **Gemma**]* What's the matter with you? |
| **Gemma** | Nothing. |
| **Mam** | Gemma's learning to play the flute. |
| **Dad** | What for? |
| **Mam** | To play it, Robbie. Why else would you learn to play a musical instrument? She's getting lessons off Mr Banerjee's grandson. |
| **Dad** | Banerjee? How old is this boy then? |
| **Mam** | Fourteen? Fifteen? |
| **Dad** | Should she be going round on her own? |
| **Mam** | It's fine, Robbie. They're all right. |
| **Dad** | I'm not happy about her going there on her own. |
| **Gemma** | You can't stop me, Dad. |
| **Dad** | What did you say? |
| **Gemma** | Mam can stop me, sure, but you can't because you're in here. |
| **Dad** | Gemma, don't talk to me like that! |
| **Gemma** | What are you doing here? |
| **Dad** | What? |
| **Mam** | Gemma. |
| **Gemma** | I don't know anyone in school whose dad's in prison. My bike was nicked the other day and Kate got it back for me. Not you, Kate did. |

| Dad | Who's Kate? |
|---|---|
| Gemma | Doesn't matter! Someone nicked my bike, but I couldn't ask you to help because you're in here. You're missing it all, Dad. The Mawr's different now, but you wouldn't know because you're in here. You get food and you're kept warm. Mam's working. She's paying the bills. She's getting the food in. She's doing what mams do, but you…! Gran called you useless. And she's right – while you're in here you're as useless as a teat on a bull! |

• • • • • • • • • • • • • • • • • • • • • • • • • • • • • • • • • • • • • • • • • • • •

**SCENE 16**

*At **Gran's**. **Gemma**, **Gran**, **Mam** and **Darren** are there.*

| Gemma | *[To the audience]* Then it all just got worse. That was my fault too. |
|---|---|
| Mam | Oh my God! I don't believe it! |
| Darren | What is it? |
| Mam | Oh my God! |
| Darren | Is it the cows? |
| Mam | Yeah. |
| Darren | Oh no! Have they gone? |
| Mam | No. Look! They're on the telly. |
| Darren | The telly?! |
| Gran | Now the world knows. |
| Darren | How? |
| Gemma | It was me. I phoned the paper. |
| Mam | Gemma? You?! |
| Gemma | I wish I hadn't. I just thought if more people knew it would help. But now they've been on the telly. We should get them all in the open, like Morris did. |

| | |
|---|---|
| **Gran** | Why? |
| **Gemma** | Mr Thomas will have seen the news. He's not thick. He'll come and round them up. Our only hope is if he sees how much everyone loves the cows, maybe he'll change his mind. |
| **Darren** | Can't we just move them to a different house every night? They'll never find them. |
| **Gran** | The cows wouldn't thank us for that, love. Your sister's right. What's the point of hiding them now? |
| **Gemma** | We should tell Mr Thomas. |
| **Gran** | They are his. |
| **Gemma** | And Defra. |
| **Mam** | Let's hope it works. |
| **Gemma** | *[To the audience]* So I went back, across the bridge and up the hill. |

**SCENE 17**

*The farm.* **Mr Thomas** *opens the door.*

| | |
|---|---|
| **Mr Thomas** | Brought the cows have you? |
| **Gemma** | We're… we're taking all the cows on to the Mawr Common tomorrow morning. We're not hiding them anymore. |
| **Mr Thomas** | Shall I tell you the irony? Mostyn doesn't want them anymore. Now this saga has been on the telly, he doesn't want them. He wants his money, of course, but not the cows. There's no other dairy farmer round here, so the quickest way I can pay him back is to take them straight to slaughter. And you all thought you were saving them. |
| **Gemma** | Well, the cows will be on the Common tomorrow morning, waiting. |
| **Mr Thomas** | Good. You can help Kate bring them all back up here. |

| | |
|---|---|
| **Gemma** | I'd better go home. |
| **Mr Thomas** | I think you should. |
| **Gemma** | *[To the audience]* But I didn't. I went round to Mostyn's farm. |

*Mostyn's farm*

| | |
|---|---|
| **Mostyn** | You lost? |
| **Gemma** | Are you Mr Mostyn? |
| **Mostyn** | I am. |
| **Gemma** | My gran's got one of your cows. |
| **Mostyn** | You mean your gran stole one of Nigel Thomas's cows. They're not mine. |
| **Gemma** | The cow was Kate's to give. |
| **Mostyn** | What do you want? |
| **Gemma** | Why don't you give us the cows? |
| **Mostyn** | They're not mine to give. Ask Thomas to give away his cows. |
| **Gemma** | He can't. He needs the money to pay you. |
| **Mostyn** | That's right. I've got my field back. Now I want my money. And what gives you the idea that I'm in a position to give away cows? |
| **Gemma** | You're a big-time farmer. You got money. |
| **Mostyn** | *[Laughs]* That it? Flattery? Listen. Thomas was handed his farm on a plate – I started mine from scratch! So you go back down the Mawr and tell them to give Thomas back his cows, and then he can honour his debt – the debt he owes me. |
| **Gemma** | Please, Mr Mostyn. I told the papers and now I feel really bad. Please save 'em. |
| **Mostyn** | Kate Thomas was round here asking me the same thing. So |

I'll tell you what I told her – I don't want them now, girly. I want my money.

**Gemma**   It's all your fault!

**Mostyn**   What?

**Gemma**   You put Mr Thomas under pressure. Kate was only trying to save the cows. She cares, is all. If you were a cow you'd be well dead and eaten by now. My gran needs that cow and so does everyone else. You don't, you got loads. You don't live on the Mawr. You don't know what it's like. You haven't got a clue. 'Miser Mostyn' they call you – no wonder.

[*To the audience*] I screamed all the way down the hill.

● ● ● ● ● ● ● ● ● ● ● ● ● ● ● ● ● ● ● ● ● ● ● ● ● ● ● ● ● ● ● ● ● ● ● ● ● ● ● ● ● ● ● ● ● ● ●

**SCENE 19**

At home. Late. **Mam** is dealing with a pile of washing. She looks tired. **Gemma** comes in.

**Mam**   What are you doing out of bed?

**Gemma**   Thirsty, Mam – really thirsty. Came down for some water.

**Mam**   Your dad was on the phone.

**Gemma**   Oh, yeah. What did he want?

**Mam**   I think he was a bit shook up by you having a go at him.

**Gemma**   Just telling it how it is.

**Mam**   Yeah. You take after me. Do him good to hear it, 'specially coming from you. I know he's all grins when we visit and you'd think he was in a holiday camp, but he wants to be out. He ended up inside because he's gullible, Gemma. People took advantage of him. I know that now.

**Gemma**   Do I look angry, Mam?

**Mam**   Angry?

**Gemma**   Yeah, have I got an angry sort of face?

| | |
|---|---|
| **Mam** | What do you mean? |
| **Gemma** | Like Sian and Gary Tobin. They have these angry faces. Clenched like a fist. Ready to fight all the time. |
| **Mam** | No, not at all. You've got a pretty face. |
| **Gemma** | What do you do, Mam? In your job, like? |
| **Mam** | How d'you mean? |
| **Gemma** | I just want to know what you do, cos I don't know. |
| **Mam** | Well, there's not a lot to say. It's an electronics factory and I'm at the most boring end – sticking the parts in boxes as they come through. |
| **Gemma** | And what do the parts do? |
| **Mam** | Do you know what? I haven't a clue. I can't believe it. I've been working there a couple of years now and I haven't a clue! |
| **Gemma** | Why don't you ask to do something else? |
| **Mam** | Shoving things in boxes is about my level, Gem. That's why I nag you about school and homework, because, I tell you, you don't want a job like mine when you leave school – rots your brain. There are days when I feel like a robot. |
| **Gemma** | What were you doing before? |
| **Mam** | Dole, when I first left school. Then I had a job in a canteen at a car factory where I met your dad. I enjoyed that. |
| **Gemma** | What happened? |
| **Mam** | You happened. |
| **Gemma** | Sorry. |
| **Mam** | I didn't enjoy it that much, Gemma. I was happy to be pregnant. |
| **Gemma** | I bet you could do something else, Mam. |

| | |
|---|---|
| **Mam** | What's all this about? |
| **Gemma** | Nothing, Mam. Just don't like the thought of you not liking your job. |
| **Mam** | Can't be too choosy round here, Gemma. |
| **Gemma** | Do you think it'll help, Mam – taking the cows on the Common? |
| **Mam** | No idea, love. Come on now. Off to bed! |
| **Gemma** | OK. Love you, Mam. |
| **Mam** | *[As **Gemma** is leaving]* Gem. I should have told you before, but… your Dad… he's coming home next weekend. |
| **Gemma** | You never said. |
| **Mam** | Yeah, well… 'Reintegration leave' it's called. Just for the weekend. |
| **Gemma** | It's crap timing. |
| **Mam** | Let's all just have an easy time. We got enough on our plates as it is, so let's just make the most of it, please. |
| **Gemma** | OK, Mam. |

● ● ● ● ● ● ● ● ● ● ● ● ● ● ● ● ● ● ● ● ● ● ● ● ● ● ● ● ● ● ● ● ● ● ● ● ● ● ● ● ● ● ● ● ● ● ● ● ● ● ● ● ● ● ● ●

**SCENE 20**

| | |
|---|---|
| **Gemma** | *[To the audience]* So, all the cows got brought to the Common. |
| | *The cows and community gather on the Common. There's someone with a sign, 'SAVE THE BRYN MAWR DOZEN'.* |
| **Gran** | It's like when we used to have fêtes here. |
| **Morris** | It's like I've always had her. She's got such a gentle temperament. |
| **Gran** | If I could have Jane in the lounge of an evening, I would. |
| | *Sound of a megaphone.* |

SCENE 20

ACT TWO

71

| Policeman | *[Speaks through a megaphone]* Can I have your attention, please? These cows are not allowed on this public ground. |
|---|---|
| | ***Kate** and **Mr Thomas** are with the **policeman**.* |
| | They were moved from their farm without the correct notification. So by order of the Department of Environment they have to be inspected. We don't want a fuss. Just let Mr Thomas check them over. |
| **Mr Thomas** | Come on then, Donna. |
| **Morris** | Looking after her, I am. She's fine. |
| **Mr Thomas** | I need to inspect the cow. |
| **Morris** | Don't take her off me. |
| **Gran** | Morris. |
| **Mr Thomas** | What have you been feeding her? |
| **Morris** | Hay and grass. Took her here the other day to stretch her legs and have a feed. |
| **Mr Thomas** | Seems fine. |
| **Morris** | That's what I told you. |
| | ***Mr Thomas** goes to the **policeman** and takes the megaphone.* |
| **Mr Thomas** | *[Speaks through the megaphone]* These cows were all taken from my farm without permission. The police say I could press charges… |
| | No harm seems to have come to them, but you took them. You can bring them back. So here's the deal. If they're all up at my farm by the end of today, I won't take matters any further. |
| | ***Mr Thomas** and the **policeman** go, leaving **Kate**.* |
| **Gemma** | Sorry. It was me that rung the papers. |
| **Kate** | Was it? Glad it's over and finished with, to be honest. |
| **Gemma** | Did he mean it last night about the cows going to slaughter? |

| Kate | Don't know. He has to find a new buyer, or take them to market. |
| | *There is a hefty moo from **Donna**. **Gran** comes running.* |
| Gran | Kate! Kate! |
| Gemma | What is it, Gran? |
| Gran | It's Donna – there's something wrong. |
| Kate | How d'you mean? |
| Gran | I don't rightly know. |

• • • • • • • • • • • • • • • • • • • • • • • • • • • • • • • • • • • • • • • • • •

## SCENE 21

| | *They get to **Donna**.* |
| Morris | What is it? |
| Kate | She's too early, I think she's ready to calve. |
| Gran | Oh, love. |
| Kate | But something's not right. I need my dad. |
| | *It gets dark. People bring lamps. **Mr Thomas** arrives.* |
| Gran | Thank you for coming. |
| Mr Thomas | *[To **Donna**]* Easy girl. |
| Kate | Dad, I– |
| Mr Thomas | They're your cows. Get cleaned up and find out what's wrong. *[To the watchers]* We'll need more straw. |
| | ***Kate** has put on a long glove.* |
| | Reach in as far as you can, and tell me what you feel. |
| Kate | I can feel a foot. |
| Mr Thomas | Can you feel a calf's head? |
| Kate | No. |

| | |
|---|---|
| **Mr Thomas** | OK. Try and pull the foot round. Don't worry about hurting her – it'll only make it easier. |
| **Kate** | I've shifted it a bit. |
| **Mr Thomas** | Now try again to feel for the head, or the nose of the calf. |
| **Kate** | There's something. Yeah, it's the head. |
| **Mr Thomas** | Now you've got to try and bring the head round and reach the other leg. |
| **Kate** | OK. The head's facing forward. |
| **Mr Thomas** | Now go as far as you can. Pull the other leg round. |
| **Kate** | I can't. |
| **Mr Thomas** | You can. |
| **Kate** | Take over, Dad! |
| **Mr Thomas** | No. Try again. |
| **Kate** | Got the knee. |
| **Mr Thomas** | Good. Straighten it and pull her round. Easy girl… Make sure the head isn't tipping back. It should be between both hooves. |
| **Gran** | There they are. I can see the hooves. |
| **Morris** | Where? |
| **Kate** | Step back, Morris. |
| **Mr Thomas** | She'll take over, Kate. Let her go. |
| | *They step back and the calf slips out.* |
| **Morris** | Good girl. |
| | *The calf is manipulated to life by the whole community.* |
| **Kate** | Thanks, Dad. I couldn't have done it without you. |
| **Gran** | You better clean up, love. |

| | |
|---|---|
| **Kate** | Thanks Lilly. |
| | *She leaves.* |
| **Gran** | What about the calf? What do we need to do? |
| **Mr Thomas** | Donna will look after her. She's done it before. But she'll need some fodder. I'll drop some round tomorrow. |
| **Gran** | But… don't you want them up at the farm? |
| **Mr Thomas** | Not the best time to be moving a cow and her calf. Better they stay here for now. That doesn't mean all the cows. Just these two. She did really well. |
| **Kate** | *[Returning]* Yeah, Donna was great. So patient. |
| **Mr Thomas** | I meant you. Proud of you, I am. |
| **Kate** | Sorry, Dad. I'm sorry I made such a mess of things. |
| **Mr Thomas** | Oh, it was already a mess, Kate. Your grandad was right. I don't have the stomach for farming. I should have done something about it long ago. |
| **Kate** | He did say that, Dad, but that's not all… |
| **Mr Thomas** | What he said was nothing I didn't already know. |
| **Kate** | No. He also said that you could bend wood with your hands, and that you had green fingers. Said you'd make a fine carpenter or gardener. |
| **Mr Thomas** | Wish he'd said it to me. |
| **Kate** | I told it to you wrong on purpose. I was mad at you. |
| **Mr Thomas** | I tell you what was peculiar. Seeing those cows on the Mawr Common. It triggered a memory – me taking cows down here as a boy, with my dad. Then they built the estate and it wasn't safe to bring them down here anymore. |
| **Kate** | The cows! We need to take them back. |
| **Mr Thomas** | They'll keep till the morning. I still need to sell those twelve cows. |

| Gran | Thirteen now. |
| --- | --- |
| Mr Thomas | Aye, thirteen. I could take them to market but the cost of getting them there isn't going to help. I could go cap in hand to Mostyn, though he was pretty annoyed with me. |
| Gran | How much would we need to buy them? |
| Gemma | We could have a farm, right here. |
| Mr Thomas | Thousands. About eight of them were just going to pay back the debt I owe him. So I've not much choice. |
| Gemma | Can we keep them till the end of the week? |
| Mr Thomas | They might as well stay… Till the weekend. |
| Gran | Let's have a fête! Like in the old days. Give them a proper send-off. |
| Morris | That's a great idea! |
| Mam | Let's do it! |
| Darren | Mam, what's a fête? |
| Mam | It's a big party, son. |

• • • • • • • • • • • • • • • • • • • • • • • • • • • • • • • • • • • • • • • • • • • • • • • •

## SCENE 22

*All the preparations begin for the fête.* **Dad** *arrives.*

| Gemma | Dad! |
| --- | --- |
| Dad | All right, Gemma. |
| Darren | Dad, try some of Jane's cheese. |
| Dad | Who's Jane? |
| Gemma | Dad! |
| Dad | Just joking. |
| Darren | She does milk too. It's amazing. |
| Gran | Welcome home, Robbie. |

| | |
|---|---|
| **Gemma** | I love milk, me. |
| **Dad** | Thanks, Lilly. |
| **Roger** | Hello Robbie! Saw through the bars, then? |
| **Mam** | Roger! |
| **Dad** | It's all right. Just having a joke, eh Rodge? |
| **Roger** | Course I was. |
| **Dad** | By the way, what happened to my Tom Jones? |
| **Gemma** | Sorry, it was– |
| **Mam** | Knocked him over dusting, I did. |
| **Dad** | Oh well, never mind… Things change, eh? Cows on the Mawr? Who'd have thought? |
| **Gemma** | Not for much longer. |
| **Dad** | What's next? Elephants? |
| **Darren** | You never know. We're having a Hindu festival today too! |
| **Gemma** | It's called Holi! |
| **Darren** | Gem, I found out who did it – who beat up Karuna. |
| **Gemma** | Who? |
| **Darren** | Tobin brothers. I heard them laughing about it. |
| **Gemma** | Shouldn't we tell the police, Mam? |
| **Mam** | Yeah, we should. |
| | *She takes out her phone.* |
| **Dad** | What are you doing? |
| **Mam** | Karuna was badly beaten up, Robbie. |
| **Dad** | Listen. No son of mine's gonna be a grass. |
| **Mam** | What?! That what you learned inside, Robbie? It's OK to beat someone up and leave it alone. Look away, is it? |

| Dad | What's got into you lot? I come back and you're talking about cows and having a Hindu festival and… grassing on someone, just because them next door… |
| Gemma | Don't make it go back, Dad! Please? I love the way things are now, honest to God. We love it. If you want it to go back to the way it was then… then you might as well go back inside. |

*Dad goes off.*

| Mam | Go after him, Gem. |
| Darren | I don't want to be a grass. |
| Gemma | What's a grass, Darren? |
| Darren | Someone who tells on someone. |
| Gemma | And why's it bad? |
| Darren | Just is. No one likes a grass. |
| Gemma | What if they beat up me? Or Mam? Or Gran? |
| Darren | But what if I get called a grass? |
| Gemma | You tell 'em cows love grass. Then I'll go and sort them out. I'm gonna find Dad. |

• • • • • • • • • • • • • • • • • • • • • • • • • • • • • • • • • • • • • • • • • • • • • • •

## SCENE 23

| Gemma | *[To the audience]* He hadn't gone very far. *[Finds Dad]* Dad. Sorry. |
| Dad | I was just sneaking a quiet moment. Too many people. All my fans! |
| Gemma | Don't joke! Whenever we visited we always asked you how you were, and you'd make jokes, but you never asked how we felt having you inside… We never went anywhere or did anything, Dad, because we couldn't afford to. You made us prisoners. |

| | |
|---|---|
| **Dad** | You're right, Gem. I made things bad for you all, but that doesn't mean I didn't think about you every day, especially after your gran visited. |
| **Gemma** | Gran? When was that? |
| **Dad** | Not long after I went in. Had a proper go at me. I just couldn't bear the real picture. So I thought about a happy made-up family to stop myself going crazy. I thought about us going on a picnic – just the four of us. We'd go to a place I used to visit as a kid… |
| **Gemma** | Dad? |
| **Dad** | The sun was shining and there was a waterfall and we sat under a tree and ate the food. Me and Darren stuck our head in the water. Lovely that day… The times I thought about it. |
| **Gemma** | That wasn't made up, Dad. |
| **Dad** | I didn't think you'd remember. It was a long time ago. |
| **Gemma** | When you put your heads in the waterfall Darren said it froze his brain… |
| **Dad** | That's right. |
| **Gemma** | You wore a checked shirt and a cowboy hat. You'd done a house clearance with your mate Danny, and with the money you bought Mam a dress, and the shirt and hat for yourself. You bought me new shoes – red sandals with a flower on the strap, and you bought Darren a cowboy suit.<br><br>You tried to teach me and Darren to do handstands. You're right, Dad, it was a lovely day. |
| **Dad** | We'll go back there, love. I promise. We'll have a special day out. |
| **Gemma** | No. Somewhere else, Dad. I don't want to go back. Seaside would be nice. Just don't wear the cowboy hat. |
| **Dad** | You've all changed so much – your mam, Darren and especially you. I feel left behind and stupid, that's the thing. I feel stupid. |

| | |
|---|---|
| **Gemma** | You're not stupid, Dad. |
| **Dad** | Clever men don't go to prison, Gem. Gonna try this time. I mean it. I don't want to go back there. Ever. |
| **Gemma** | And we don't want you to. Come on, back to the fête. |
| **Dad** | Can't, Gem. Too many people. Scared. |
| **Gemma** | Come be with Mam. She's always on her own. |

*They find **Mam**.*

● ● ● ● ● ● ● ● ● ● ● ● ● ● ● ● ● ● ● ● ● ● ● ● ● ● ● ● ● ● ● ● ● ● ● ● ● ● ● ● ● ● ● ●

**SCENE 24**

*Gemma and **Kate**.*

| | |
|---|---|
| **Gemma** | *[To the audience]* The one person missing was Cowgirl herself. I went to find her. She was up the hill. Sitting on a gate. |
| | *[To **Kate**]* You coming to join in? |
| **Kate** | I'm better with cows than people. |
| **Gemma** | They named Donna's calf Kate. |
| **Kate** | That's nice. |
| **Gemma** | How's your dad? |
| **Kate** | Not great. He helped me apply for a City Farm grant. He's good like that. |
| **Gemma** | But the cows will have to be sold before then, won't they? |
| **Kate** | Yeah. How's your dad? |
| **Gemma** | It's weird having him back. He doesn't like crowds either. Or the outside. Come on then, hop on my bike, I'll give you a croggy. |
| **Kate** | No. |
| **Gemma** | It'll be quicker. |
| **Kate** | No! |

| | |
|---|---|
| **Gemma** | Why? |
| **Kate** | I can't ride a bike. All right! Don't you dare laugh, Gemma. |
| **Gemma** | I'm not laughing. You don't have to ride it – I can cycle with you on the saddle. |
| **Kate** | No. Hang on a minute. What's going on down there? |
| **Gemma** | *[To the audience]* I looked down at the Bryn Mawr. I couldn't work it out at first. It was like some sort of creature moving up the hill towards us. I'll never forget it. The kites were leading the way, and the cows were plodding behind. Then after the cows were people, hundreds of people. It was if the whole of the Bryn Mawr had decided to take a stroll at the same time, snaking all the way up Craig-y-Nos Hill. |
| **Kate** | Hope they're not all expecting a cup of tea. |
| | *The whole cast hold milk cartons. **Gran** puts one down. **Gemma** picks it up and looks at it.* |
| | What is it? |
| **Gemma** | It's money. It's full of money. |
| | *Others come and lay their cartons down.* |
| | They're all full of money. |
| **Gran** | And not just from the Mawr. From town and all over the valleys. |
| | ***Sian** brings one and gives it to **Gemma**. There is a nod between them.* |
| **Kate** | How much? |
| **Gemma** | Enough? |
| **Gran** | Enough to buy your dad's cows. |
| **Gemma** | Enough to start a City Farm? |
| **Gran** | I think so. |
| **Morris** | We'll have to clear the Common of rubbish. |

| | |
|---|---|
| **Roger** | And put a fence round it. |
| **Mave** | We'll start tomorrow. |
| **Mr Banerjee** | It's blessed by Krishna. The holy herdsman. |

*There is a big celebration.*

● ● ● ● ● ● ● ● ● ● ● ● ● ● ● ● ● ● ● ● ● ● ● ● ● ● ● ● ● ● ● ● ● ● ● ● ● ● ●

## SCENE 25

*Gemma and Kate pull away. Gemma has her bike.*

| | |
|---|---|
| **Gemma** | *[To Kate]* Get on. |
| **Kate** | All right. Where we going? |
| **Gemma** | Who knows? Two cowgirls together. We could go anywhere. Hold on tight! |

*Off they go. Screaming.*

**The End.**

# TEACHING AND LEARNING ACTIVITIES

The structured and challenging approaches, outlined in the detailed scheme of work, enable learners to develop critical thinking, skills in Reading and Writing, Speaking and Listening and independent learning. The use of a wide range of drama techniques and active learning approaches are all designed to raise standards in English.

### Structured learning and critical analysis
Through the use of structured learning, students:
- develop critical thinking, independent learning and transferable skills
- analyse writers' complex techniques and skills
- understand writers' intentions and choices of language, structures and ideas
- analyse the different contributions made by novelists, playwrights, directors, narrators
- analyse images, drama and literary techniques
- use drama techniques that enable learners to visualize, physicalize and articulate complex ideas and concepts
- understand texts in a cultural and historical context
- develop contexts and techniques to produce high-level responses and skills.

### Analytical writing at KS3 and GCSE
The learning approaches, outlined in the scheme of work, enable students to develop their ability to write about literary and dramatic techniques and use evidence from the text to back up their ideas. Integrated within the work are, therefore, suggestions for further analytical work, assessment opportunities and related activities. It is important that the drama activities are not seen as separate from these as they should complement each other. Discussions and written work should be directly informed by drama work resulting in a more detailed analysis and understanding of the text and of the dramatic/literary process.

### Using the scheme of work
The use of drama conventions and textual analysis in isolation will not produce deep learning opportunities. The Teaching and Learning Activities are, therefore, developed in such a way that students are able to make progress because they are provided with the appropriate contexts and techniques to produce high-level responses and skills. Sharing such an approach with the students allows them to have an understanding of the learning process, vital if they are to become independent,

active learners. The Teaching and Learning Activities are addressed to students and teachers. Together, the 'Learning and Teaching' column and the 'Guidance and Resources' column enable teachers to plan and deliver the structured scheme of work. By addressing students directly within the 'Learning and Teaching' column, the emphasis is placed on the learning, which enables students to understand and analyse the process and consider the progress they are making in the skills identified.

Similarly, the 'Additional activities' sections are also addressed to teachers and students so that decisions can be made about how deeper learning and/or independent skills might be developed further.

While individual activities are identified within the scheme, they are often interlinked and interdependent and are best approached within the complete scheme of work. Similarly, lesson breaks are not identified, as this will be dependent on the length of lessons and nature of the learning groups involved.

A glossary defining dramatic techniques and conventions can be found at www.oxfordsecondary.co.uk/cowgirloxfordplayscripts.

## Resources

All the resources required are identified in the scheme of work. Some preparation time is needed to ensure that these are available when required. For example, the objects required for activities (flute, bike pump, leaves, tin of corned beef, bucket, box) can, when not readily available, be purchased cheaply or replaced with similar items. For ease of use, a laptop and multimedia projector will enable extracts of the text to be projected on to a screen for students to see. The Bach flute music, referenced in the script, provides the most effective music to be used during the activities, but other appropriate music without lyrics, if necessary, can be used in the places identified. Copies of the extracts from the novel and other resources can be found at www.oxfordsecondary.co.uk/cowgirloxfordplayscripts.

## Use of space

While some of the activities benefit from a more open environment that allows for a flexible use of floor space, tables and chairs, a drama studio or large space is not required. If space is limited, a classroom can easily be adjusted to enable all the activities to take place.

*Paul Bunyan and Ruth Moore*
*Title consultants and national*
*experts in Drama in English*

# 1 YOU HAVE TO CROSS A BRIDGE TO BRYN MAWR ESTATE

Establish a context and setting for the play.

| Learning and Teaching | Guidance and Resources |
|---|---|
| • Sit in a large semicircle facing the projected image of a place (see image on page 89). Identify what you can see. What sort of place is it? What features can you describe? Items that could be found in some of the houses (for example, flute, dog bowl, iron, bucket, tin of corned beef, Hindu statue, etc.) have been placed around the room. | Resources – the picture of the fictional Bryn Mawr estate should be projected throughout. www.oxfordsecondary.co.uk/ cowgirloxfordplayscripts<br><br>Props – flute, dog bowl, iron, bucket, tin of corned beef, Hindu statue |
| • The teacher will read from the novel, **'…it was all concrete and shutters – back on the Bryn Mawr estate…'** (page 7) | |
| • In pairs, decide who is 'A' and who is 'B'.<br><br>• Student A: You need to imagine that you know this place really well. You know what can be found around each street corner, who lives in the houses and what smells and sounds you will come across as you walk around the estate. Using the projected image and the text that your teacher will read before you begin, take your partner (Student B) on a Guided Tour, describing and commenting on the things that you can see around you with your 'drama eyes', smell with your 'drama nose' or hear with your 'drama ears', as you move around the space. | Resources – the picture should remain projected throughout. If it is possible to project the text at the same time, this allows the students to use both resources available. Copies of the picture can also be laminated (if possible) and one given to each pair.<br><br>If the students are unfamiliar with this drama convention, the teacher may need to model the process first. Select a student (B) and take them on a brief Guided Tour describing some of the things you 'see' and 'hear' around you to model the process. |

- Student B: You need to imagine that you have never been to this place before and know nothing about the people and homes you are about to visit. You need to keep your eyes closed while Student A holds you by the arm and guides you around the space. You need to listen to the description of the location carefully as you will be asked later to feed back to the class what you have found out.

- Before the Guided Tour begins, your teacher will provide some narration and read an extract from the novel, **'I live in the new part of the Mawr, which is a big estate stuck on to the old bit. In between is the Bryn Mawr Common, which is covered in litter and bits of furniture. You don't want to live here, I tell you. The old part of the Mawr is a bit nicer. There's rows of terraced streets, where Gran lives, and alleyways that run along the back of them. Gran has a house on one of the terraces.'** (page 7)

- Begin the Guided Tour, exploring the homes of the Bryn Mawr residents and some of the objects that can be found in them.

Before reading the extract from the novel, provide a few seconds of narration about the Bryn Mawr estate, using information the students gave when looking at the image and items from the houses.

It is helpful to project the text, to allow the students to focus on what is being said.

- When you are asked to freeze, stop quickly and keep very still and silent. Gather around your teacher. If you are Student B (Visitor), feed back to the class what you have seen with your 'drama eyes', heard with your 'drama ears' and perhaps 'smelt' as you were guided around the homes. Listen carefully to the information provided by the other students.

- This time, Student B is to take Student A on a Guided Tour, describing and commenting on the things that can be seen. The focus of the Guided Tour will this time be on the outside of the houses and the estate.

| | |
|---|---|
| • Before the second Guided Tour begins, listen carefully to your teacher narrating information about the place, using information and ideas from the feedback that has just been given. He/she will then read from the novel, **'I stopped at the top of the hill and gazed down on the twinkling lights of the Mawr estate. It seemed like a toy town, unreal.'** (page 196)<br><br>• Begin the Guided Tour, exploring the old and newer Bryn Mawr estates, the common and the surrounding streets and buildings. | The pairs need to move into a space.<br><br>Before the second Guided Tours begin, narrate information about the homes they have visited, the props they have explored and their 'tours', using information and ideas from the feedback you have just received.<br><br>Project the text and image. |
| • When you are asked to freeze, turn to see the projected text from the novel, read by the teacher, **' "The Bryn Mawr estate is often in the news for all the wrong reasons," he said. "Ask anyone on this estate and they'll tell you about petty crime, burglary, joyriders, graffiti and intimidation. One elderly lady I spoke to said she was too frightened to leave her house alone. But recently a change has come about on this estate –" '** (page 189) | Play music (e.g. Bach flute works as referenced in the novel) during the Guided Tour activity and while reading the extract from the script. |
| • Discuss the extract from the novel and the place you have explored during the Guided Tour activity. What significance might they have for the play you are about to study? | |

| **Additional activities, analysis and/or discussion** |
|---|
| 1. Discuss what the extracts from the novel suggest about the play you are about to explore. |
| 2. How has the Guided Tour activity helped you to gain an understanding of the setting and enabled you to think about the context of the play? How could the playwright and/or a film director use similar techniques to convey a sense of place and atmosphere? |
| 3. Discuss the use of props. How and why do the items begin to take on significance? |
| 4. How might the playwright or director choose to use similar techniques to those used in this activity to convey ideas and/or atmosphere to the audience? |

# 2 I Was Looking For Somewhere, But I Didn't Find It

Introduce key ideas and characters in the play.

| Learning and Teaching | Guidance and Resources |
|---|---|
| • Sit in a large semicircle facing the projected text of the opening of the play. In the centre of the semicircle is a box with a letter 'G' on its lid. The teacher reads from **'The whole cast looking at the audience.'** to **'Aaaaaah. Get away from me. Get away! Moo'** (page 5). Recorded sound effects are used to create the sounds of the cows. | It is helpful to project the text. Sound effects of real cows mooing should be used in between the reading of the text. <br><br> Prop – box (to represent Gemma's jewellery box) with artificial leaves inside |
| • The sound effect of the cows gradually changes to that of running water in a waterfall and other sounds of the countryside. | Sound effects – waterfall and countryside sounds – used throughout this activity. |
| • The teacher picks up the box and passes it to one of the students, opening it so that the leaves inside can be seen. He/she asks that the box be passed slowly around the circle so that everyone can see the box and its contents. | Props – box with artificial leaves inside |
| • The teacher will give each student a leaf-shaped piece of paper or artificial leaf and a pen. Thinking carefully about the sounds you can hear and the visual images they create in your imagination, select a phrase that you feel describes the place or a detail within it. Try to use a simile, metaphor of other literary technique (e.g. alliteration, assonance, onomatopoeia) within your descriptive phrase. Write your phrase on the leaf. | If necessary, discuss the different ways that literary techniques could be used to create a greater sense of place or more effective description. |
| • The box will be passed back round the circle. Each time a student takes hold of it, they will read out loud their phrase, written on the leaf, and then place the leaf carefully in the box. The sound effects of the waterfall will continue throughout. | Sound effects – waterfall and countryside sounds – used throughout this activity. |

- When all the phrases have been spoken and the leaves placed in the box, the teacher will close the lid and place the box in the centre of the circle before reading the following extract from the play:

  **When I was on my bike I was looking for somewhere, but I didn't find it. It was a waterfall. Dad took us there for a picnic. Dad and Darren dared each other to put their heads in the icy water. I was wearing these new sandals Dad had bought me and they got all dirty. It was a few days after that he got arrested. Mam was crying. I was crying. It was horrible. He said he'd be back, but he wasn't. They sent him to prison for petty larceny and fraud, which is a posh way of saying cheating and stealing.**

  **Well, the day after he was arrested I was putting on my new shoes and I noticed dried grass and leaves stuck to the soles. I cried. Again. Not because they were all dirty but because that was the last day everything was OK. I put the mud and leaves in this box. Just dirt, people'd say. And I just feel like, if I could find it. Go back to that place...** (page 15)

- Discuss the extract from the script and what significance it might have for the play as a whole. What do we know about the character (Gemma) who owns the box?

It is helpful to project the text.

## Additional activities, analysis and/or discussion

1. Discuss what you understood and felt about the contrast between the Bryn Mawr estate and the waterfall/rural sounds. How might these ideas be developed throughout the play?

2. What significance do the waterfall and its location have and why is Gemma trying to find it?

3. Using all the descriptive phrases that have been projected or collated, create a collective poem by placing each phrase on a new line and rearranging them until you feel you have created an effective poem. Think carefully about the order of the lines and the different effects that might be created by beginning a new stanza and/or placing different phrases next to each other.

# 3 What Am I Supposed To Do About It?

Explore the opening of the play and the techniques used to introduce the characters and key ideas.

| Learning and Teaching | Guidance and Resources |
|---|---|
| • You will be working in a small group of between two and four students. Each group is given a short section from the opening of the play (see extracts below).<br><br>**Extract 1 (two people)**: (pages 5–6)<br>*From* Aaaaaah! Get away.<br>*to* Oh.<br><br>**Extract 2 (three people)**: (pages 6–7)<br>*From* It doesn't start in cartons, you know.<br>*to* Rude cow.<br><br>**Extract 3 (three people)**: (pages 7–8)<br>*From* Mam?<br>*to* Cowgirl. I like that.<br><br>**Extract 4 (two people)**: (pages 8–9)<br>*From* I'd been in the countryside…<br>*to* …because she was the only one who you didn't snarl at or bite.<br><br>**Extract 5 (four people)**: (pages 9–10)<br>*From* Do you want something?<br>*to* He's in his bedroom playing the flute.<br><br>**Extract 6 (two people)**: (pages 10–11)<br>*From* Oh. Gran, I better be going.<br>*to* Terrible.<br><br>**Extract 7 (two people)**: (page 11)<br>*From* We all go down the post office as a mob…<br>*to* I hate cows. | Copies of the scripts can be used for this activity but the teacher might find it useful to reproduce the extracts on sheets of A4 paper or card. If these are colour-coded, it is easy for the teacher to see which of the extracts different groups are working on and the chronological order can more easily be maintained.<br><br>By exploring these extracts, the students begin to select and analyse information from the text. They also begin to take a real interest in the material and want to know more. By Action Reading the extracts, they have to consider some of the initial issues that directors and actors need to address.<br><br>If the students are not used to working in this way, the teacher will need to explain and, if necessary, model what a Digital Video Clip technique is. He/she will also need to explain what Spect-acting means (see page 93). |

**Extract 8 (two people)**: (pages 11–12)
*From* What's a cow ever done to you?
*to* Great. Totally fab'lous.

**Extract 9 (three people)**: (pages 12–13)
*From* So I goes home.
*to* Don't you ever give me that lip, Gemma.

**Extract 10 (three people)**: (pages 13–14)
*From* Yeah!
*to* Creep.

During the time that students are 'rehearsing' their Digital Video Clips, the teacher will need to stop them at regular intervals to focus on the Still Images and the ways that character, use of space and tension are being explored.

- In your group, produce a short Digital Video Clip of your extract. To do this, you begin with a Still Image, followed by an Action Reading of the script (speaking the lines, adding gestures and movements) and then freeze at the end in a final Still Image. You need to discuss the script and search for clues about the characters, story and setting in order to produce an accurate Action Reading of the extract.

After a few minutes of 'rehearsal' stop the students (by counting them down from 5 to 1) and ask them to show the Still Images. Once they have all frozen, ask them to sharpen the pictures to show the tension. Insist that everyone remains completely still.

- As a class, produce your Digital Video Clips as Rolling Theatre. Music is used to guide you. All the groups freeze in their initial Still Image and then the first group unfreezes, completes the Action Reading and then freezes again. When they freeze, the next group knows that they can begin. This continues with all the groups producing their Digital Video Clip, until all groups have shown their pieces.

Position the groups around the room according to the order of the extracts.

Play music (e.g. Bach flute works) at the start, end and in between each extract.

- When you are not presenting your Digital Video Clip, you can become a Spect-actor. This means that while your body remains frozen in the Still Image, your head can turn to follow the action so that you can see and hear the work of the other groups. You should remain in your place, in order for all the groups to freeze in their final Still Image at the end.

Remind students of the nature of Spect-acting and the importance of freezing in the final Still Images at the end of the Rolling Theatre.

- The teacher reads the next section from the play:
  *Gemma in her room. She gets out a box.*
  **All right, you're not to laugh. When I was on my bike I was looking for somewhere, but I didn't find it. It was a waterfall. Dad took us there for a picnic. Dad and Darren dared each other to put their heads in the icy water. I was wearing these new sandals Dad had bought me and they got all dirty. It was a few days after that he got arrested. Mam was crying. I was crying. It was horrible. He said he'd be back, but he wasn't. They sent him to prison for petty larceny and fraud, which is a posh way of saying cheating and stealing.**
  **Well, the day after he was arrested I was putting on my new shoes and I noticed dried grass and leaves stuck to the soles. I cried. Again. Not because they were all dirty but because that was the last day everything was OK. I put the mud and leaves in this box. Just dirt, people'd say. And I just feel like, if I could find it. Go back to that place...** (page 15)

By rereading the extract, used in Activity 2, at the point when it actually appears in the play, the students are encouraged to make links between the activities and ideas. The extract also helps them to develop their understanding of Gemma's character before completing the Role on the Object activity below.

- Sit in a large circle. Your teacher will place the wooden box, used in Activity 2, in the circle to represent the character of Gemma.

- Use the Role on the Object technique to explore her character. To do this you need to identify what you know about Gemma from the extracts and your understanding of the play so far. Choose a word you think best describes her. Your teacher will write this word on a piece of card and give it to you. Place your word on or near the box, thinking carefully where you might place it. If you are confident that the word is an accurate description of her character at this stage of the play and have evidence from the text to support this, place it on or close to the box. If you are less confident about the word and your evidence, place it at a distance.

Resources – pens and small pieces of card

Prop – box with artificial leaves inside

Use the Role on the Object technique throughout the work to explore the different characters. At different stages in the play, new words can be added and previous choices discussed. A permanent display of the ideas produced here can prove a useful prompt and recap tool, as well as providing a valuable resource when planning written responses to the text.

- Your teacher will place a stick (cattle stick) in the circle to represent Kate. Repeat the Role on the Object exercise (above) to explore the character of Kate.

Prop – stick

## Additional activities, analysis and/or discussion

1.  What techniques have been used by the playwright to introduce the audience to the key ideas and characters? What techniques would a director and/or actors use in these scenes? How did you use space, gestures, tone and facial expressions during the Digital Video Clip?

2.  Discuss how the writer has used dramatic techniques and linguistic, grammatical or structural features to achieve effects and engage and influence the audience.

3.  How might the playwright further explore/develop the differences and similarities between Gemma and Kate?

# 4 COWGIRLS TOGETHER. WE COULD GO ANYWHERE

Investigate key scenes and analyse the different techniques the playwright has used to show the strong influence that particular characters have.

| Learning and Teaching | Guidance and Resources |
|---|---|
| ● You will be working in a small group of between three and seven students. Each group is given an extract from the play (see extracts below).<br><br>**Extract 1 (four people)**: (pages 15–18)<br>*From* Hiya, Gem.<br>*to* I didn't think she'd turn up, but she's a woman of her word.<br><br>**Extract 2 (six people)**: (pages 18–20)<br>*From* Kate, right?<br>*to* My own flesh and blood.<br><br>**Extract 3 (seven people)**: (pages 20–22)<br>From **Kate** slings **Ryan** *over her shoulder.*<br>*to* And she won't believe you, anyway.<br><br>**Extract 4 (five people)**: (pages 22–24)<br>*From* **Kate** *is hosing the floor.*<br>*to* Kept the grass down lovely. | Copies of the scripts can be used for this activity but the teacher might find it useful to reproduce the extracts on sheets of A4 paper or card. If these are colour-coded, it is easy for the teacher to see which of the extracts different groups are working on and the chronological order can more easily be maintained.<br><br>By exploring these extracts, the students begin to select and analyse information from the text. They also begin to take a real interest in the material and want to know more. By Action Reading the extracts, they have to consider some of the initial issues that directors and actors need to address. |

**Extract 5 (four people)**: (pages 26–28)
*From* My bike! Where's my bike?
*to* Thanks. See you, Gran.

**Extract 6 (three people)**: (pages 29–31)
*From* No bike meant walking to the shops on Saturday.
*to* Leave it. We'll get it later.

If the students are not used to working in this way, the teacher will need to explain and, if necessary, model what a Digital Video Clip technique is. He/she will also need to explain what Spect-acting means.

During the time that students are 'rehearsing' their Digital Video Clips, the teacher will need to stop them at regular intervals to focus on the Still Images and the ways that character, use of space and tension are being explored.

- In your group, produce a short Digital Video Clip of your extract. To do this, you begin with a Still Image, followed by an Action Reading of the script and then freeze at the end in a final Still Image. You need to discuss the script and search for clues about the characters, story and setting in order to produce an accurate Action Reading of the extract.

After a few minutes of 'rehearsal' stop the students (by counting them down from 5 to 1) and ask them to show the Still Images. Once they have all frozen, ask them to sharpen the pictures to show the tension. Insist that everyone remains completely still.

- As a class, produce your Digital Video Clips as Rolling Theatre. Music is used to guide you. All the groups freeze in their initial Still Image and then the first group unfreezes, completes the Action Reading and then freezes again. When they freeze, the next group knows that they can begin. This continues with all the groups producing their Digital Video Clip, until all groups have shown their pieces.

- When you are not presenting your Digital Video Clip, you can become a Spect-actor. This means that while your body remains frozen in the Still Image, your head can turn to follow the action so that you can see and hear the work of the other groups. You should remain in your place, in order for all the groups to freeze in their final Still Image at the end.

Position the groups round the room according to the order of the extracts.

Play music at the start, end and in between each extract.

Remind students of the nature of Spect-acting and the importance of freezing in the final Still Images at the end of the Rolling Theatre.

- Reflecting on the extract that you have just produced as a Digital Video Clip, you now need to 'Distil' the extract to one Still Image and accompanying word or line.

- To do this, you need to discuss your extract as a group and decide which moment best shows a character's positive/strong influence in the scene. Use your Still Image to show how this has been achieved. For example, in the first extract when Kate says to the teacher, 'I made sure she didn't miss her first lesson and this is all the thanks I get', a Still Image could be devised to show the control that Kate not only has physically but also her ability to control the situation verbally as well.

By discussing and producing the Still Images the students have to think carefully about the text extracts and the playwright's techniques.

Stop the students (by counting them down from 5 to 1) while they are 'rehearsing' and ask them to show their Still Images. Once they have all frozen, ask them to sharpen the pictures to show the tension.

- As a class, produce your Still Images and accompanying lines of text/words as Rolling Theatre. Music is used to guide you.

- Once the Images have been presented, the teacher will select one of the groups and stand between two of the characters in the Still Image.

When Naming the Space, the teacher should actually stand in that space so that the students can visualize it.

- Using the Naming the Space technique, you need to think about a specific word that best describes the space between the two characters. You might suggest various alternatives, such as, 'The space of fear, the space of understanding, the space of ignorance…'.

- The teacher will introduce three separate pieces of card with a character's name printed on them (Gemma, Gran and Kate) and will place them on the floor in the centre of the Still Image.

- Place each Character card into the scene according to the influence that you feel the playwright has given the character and who/what you feel she influences. To do this, you need to consider what influence the character has, even if they are not in the actual scene. If she has a strong positive influence, then you would place the card at the centre of the Still Image and/or close to a particular character or action that you feel she has the most influence on. If she has less influence than another character, you might move the character card away slightly and if you feel she has no influence, then you would move the card away from the Still Image altogether.

- Justify your choices, using evidence from the text to support your ideas. Discuss the positioning as a class. Throughout this discussion, other students should demonstrate the position they feel is most appropriate by moving and Placing the Characters and justifying their choice.

The teacher might need to model this activity by asking specific questions about the characters. For example in the first extract, a discussion about whether Gran has a positive influence in that scene (on Gemma for example) even when she is not there can take place before deciding where to place the 'Gran' card. Similarly, a discussion can take place about whether Kate's influence in this scene is actually on Gemma, rather than Sian or the teacher, and so the 'Kate' card could be placed near to Gemma. Evidence from the text should be given to support all the comments.

Resources – three character cards ('Gemma', 'Kate' and 'Gran') for each group

- Return to your group and the Still Image that you produced from your extract. The teacher will provide each group with the three character cards (Gemma, Gran and Kate). Recreate your Still Image, but this time place the character cards in your own Still Image by discussing as a group the influence that you feel the characters have in your particular scene and Still Image.

Make sure that the groups are still positioned around the room according to the order of the extracts.

- Share your Still Image and comments about Placing the Characters with the whole class.

| | |
|---|---|
| **Additional activities, analysis and/or discussion** | |

1. How did the Rolling Theatre and Distilling activities help you to analyse and understand the characters and the playwright's techniques?

2. How does the playwright explore the influence that the characters have in the play? How does he explore the different perceptions of strength, weakness, unity and disunity in the play and the audience's understanding of it? What universal ideas are explored?

3. What techniques could be used by a playwright to indicate the influence that a particular character has on an event, character or scene, even when they are not actually in that scene?

4. Read and discuss Act 1 Scene 15 (pages 32–38) as a whole class before moving on to the next activity.

# 5 WE'RE ALL HELPING

Investigate and analyse the techniques the playwright uses in a pivotal scene where characters and events are seen to change, and explore the tensions in the scene and play.

| **Learning and Teaching** | **Guidance and Resources** |
|---|---|
| ● As a class, read Act 1 Scene 15 *from 'There's a crowd of neighbours round Gran's yard'* (page 32) *to* 'a useless bloke in prison and a mam with a cow in her back yard. Happy days' (page 38). | It is helpful to project the text and have individual copies of the texts for the students. |
| ● Discuss as a class why this could be described as a pivotal scene in relation to the events and the characters' reactions to them. | |
| ● You will be working in a small group of three or four students. Each group is given an extract from Act 1 Scene 15. Reflecting on the extract that you have been given, you need to identify the most significant or pivotal moment in your extract. Discuss your extract as a group and decide which line/action has the most impact on the audience in terms of demonstrating that something significant has been said or done. | The scene can be divided into different size extracts depending on the size of the class. |

| | |
|---|---|
| ● As a group, produce a Digital Video Clip of the chosen line from your extract. Begin with a Still Image, followed by an Action Reading of the line and then freeze at the end in a final Still Image. | By discussing and producing the Digital Video Clips the students have to think carefully about the text extracts and the playwright's techniques. |
| ● Discuss as a class the meaning of 'subtext' and 'inference' and how the lines that are actually being said by the characters, or their actions, in Act 1 Scene 15 might reveal issues or 'truths' that are not said or shown directly to the audience.<br><br>● For example, when Morris offers to build the cow a shelter, the audience is presented with the challenge that Morris is a different character from what they first thought. The subtext of his line, 'I'll build her a shelter' could be 'This cow has helped to show that I am capable of showing a good side and being part of this community. You've got me wrong.' | Specific examples may be required so that reference can be made to the evidence in the text and the playwright's techniques and intentions. |
| ● As a group, discuss the line that you selected and what subtext is suggested by it.<br><br>● Produce a Digital Video Clip of the 'unseen' or subtext. Begin with a Still Image, followed by an Action Reading of the subtext (the 'hidden' text, actions and truths) and then freeze at the end in a final Still Image. When developing your Still Images, consider what ideas this subtext would suggest. You could choose to present a symbolic image, such as a character representing Morris standing with his arms open to a group of people, rather than reproducing the characters' positions and/or actions on stage. | The teacher will need to explain and, if necessary, model this process. He/she might need to explain how a Still Image can be used to present a symbolic idea (creating shapes and using space and positioning to show fear, power, etc.). Stop the students (by counting them down from 5 to 1) while they are 'rehearsing' and ask them to show their Still Images. |

- As a class, produce your Digital Video Clips as Rolling Theatre, incorporating both the 'seen' and the 'unseen' (text and subtext) lines and Still Images into the process.

- All the groups freeze in their initial Still Image and then the first group unfreezes, completes the Action Reading of their chosen, significant line from their extract and then freezes again.

- The same group then merges into the Still Image that is going to begin their Digital Video Clip of the subtext or the 'unseen'. They unfreeze, presenting the subtext and then freeze again in the final Still Image. When they freeze for the second time, the next group knows that they can begin.

- This continues with all the groups producing their Digital Video Clips of the significant lines (seen text and actions) and then the subtext (unseen text and actions), until all groups have shown their pieces.

- When you are not presenting your Digital Video Clip, you can become a Spect-actor. You should remain in your place, in order for all the groups to freeze in their final Still Image at the end.

Position the groups round the room according to the order of the extracts they were given from Act 1 Scene 15.

Play music at the start, end and in between each Digital Video Clip, allowing time for the groups to merge from one Still Image to another.

Remind students of the nature of Spect-acting and the importance of freezing in the final Still Images at the end of the Rolling Theatre.

- Sit in a large semicircle facing the projected diagram of the motorway bridge (see below).

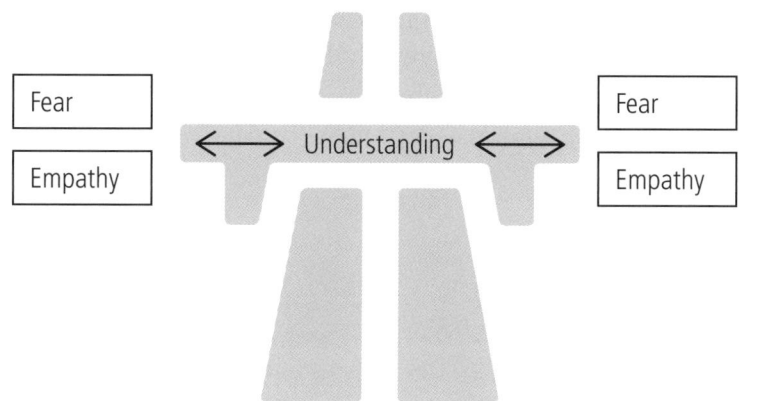

| Fear |
| Empathy |

←→ Understanding ←→

| Fear |
| Empathy |

As with the Role on the Object technique, this diagram can be used throughout the work to explore the different characters, events and ideas. At different stages in the play, changes can be made and previous choices discussed. Discussion can then take place about the techniques used by the playwright to explore the 'journey' that characters are on throughout the play and what they are influenced or affected by.

- As a class, discuss what is known so far about the play and the characters. Discuss what lies at either side of the bridge (e.g. countryside and town, age and youth, selfishness and selflessness, community and individuals) and add this to the diagram.

- Identify on the diagram, using sticky notes or annotations, where particular characters would be placed at this stage in the play, in relation to the journey that they might be taking (from fear to understanding to empathy). Explain your decision using evidence from the text. Events or actions can be identified on the diagram in the same way.

## Additional activities, analysis and/or discussion

1. Discuss why Act 1 Scene 15 could be described as a pivotal scene in the play. What techniques does the playwright use to explore the changes that take place? What causes the changes in this scene and what are the intended effects on the audience?

2. Discuss how Activity 5 has helped you to analyse the subtexts of the play. What techniques has the playwright used to build tension and to suggest that there are hidden truths and thoughts that the audience needs to understand?

3. Return to the Role on the Objects (box and stick) for Gemma and Kate from Activity 3 and add words that you would use to describe the characters at this point in the play. Discuss any changes, using evidence from the text to support your comments. Explore the techniques the playwright has used to present these changes.

4. As a class, read and discuss Act 1 Scenes 16 and 17 before moving on to the next activity.

# 6 We've Talking To Do

Explore the different dilemmas that the characters face and present an argument effectively.

| Learning and Teaching | Guidance and Resources |
|---|---|
| ● Sit in a large semicircle facing the projected text of the opening of Act 1 Scene 18. <br><br> *From At **Gran's**. **Kate** is there.* <br><br> *to* Kate's dad knows a cow is missing. <br><br> ● Using your knowledge of the play and the dilemmas that the characters face, think about the arguments and the solutions that might be raised at the meeting at Gran's house. | It is helpful to project the text. <br><br><br> As a class, recap on the events and problems on the farm that have led to the dilemmas that Kate and the community face. |
| ● Using the Meeting Convention, you are going to contribute your ideas and arguments to the meeting at Gran's house, using evidence from the text and your own ideas. Discuss with the person next to you some of the arguments that could be presented in preparation for the meeting. <br><br> ● The Teacher in Role as Gran begins the meeting and explains the purpose of the gathering by reading the following: <br> *It's really good of you all to come round here this afternoon. I think you all know by now that Kate's dad knows a cow is missing. He's blown his top and got straight on the phone to cut a deal with Mostyn. So – we've got talking to do. What can we do?* | Time will be needed to prepare arguments and consider the roles that will be adopted at the meeting. <br><br><br> Prop – an item of clothing or object (hat, scarf, walking stick) can be used to indicate when the teacher is in role and removed when he/she is not in role. |

- Listening carefully to 'Gran' and the views of the others at the meeting, present your ideas and case. At different stages in the meeting, new problems and/or solutions will arise that you will need to be able to respond to. Once the discussion has taken place, the Teacher in Role as Gran will draw the meeting to a close, using lines selected from this scene in the play and conclude with the following line from the play:
**We want the whole dozen down here, on the estate. It's all hush-hush though. (page 42)**

Remind the students that they will need to listen carefully to the views of others and decide how they can best present their case.

The Teacher in Role as Gran will need to chair the meeting by provoking responses and arguments. Information and lines from the script itself can be used to prompt discussion and move towards a conclusion.

## Additional activities, analysis and/or discussion

1. How did the Meeting Convention activity help you to analyse and understand the significance of Act 1 Scene 18? How did this activity also help you to explore the methods used by the playwright to present the different characters and issues?

2. As a class, read Act 1 Scene 18, when the meeting takes place at Gran's house. Returning to the idea explored in Activity 4, discuss the three female characters of Kate, Gemma and Gran. What strong or positive influence do they have in this scene and throughout the play?

3. Read and discuss Act 2 Scenes 1, 2 and 3 as a whole class before moving on to the next activity. Return to the Role on the Object (box and stick) for Gemma and Kate from Activity 3 and the motorway bridge diagram from Activity 5 to help explore these scenes and the techniques used by the playwright to present the characters and their journeys.

# 7 You Didn't Try, Dad. You Can't Stop Me, Dad

Analyse the motivation of the characters and identify the skills required by the playwright and director in presenting the characters' motivations.

| Learning and Teaching | Guidance and Resources |
|---|---|
| ● Sit in a large semicircle facing the projected text of the opening of Act 2 Scene 10: <br><br> *From* I went up the farm and found Kate sitting in the road. <br><br> *to* Good fun, is it? Where are they? | It is helpful to project the text. |
| ● Members of the class are given the roles of Gemma, Kate and Mr Thomas. Sculpt them into the scene at this point. You will need to consider their frozen position, facial expressions and gestures. Other members of the class might adjust the positions until a final Sculpture is agreed. | Ensure that the sculpted positions are supported with evidence from the text. Give value to the different positions offered by explaining that the director at different points in the scene could have used the positions. |
| ● Your teacher takes the place of Mr Thomas and demonstrates the Action Narration technique by clapping his/her hands (directing that all the actors should freeze at that point) and then saying what the character (Mr Thomas) is going to do next and why. For example, your teacher could say 'I am going to look straight into Gemma's and then Kate's eyes to make it clear that I know what harm they have caused and how angry and upset I am.' Your teacher then claps his/her hands again to indicate that the actors in role can come to life. He/she looks at Gemma and then Kate and says the next line, 'What are you going to solve doing this?' | This activity needs to remain tightly structured. Work through the process in stages so that the students fully understand the technique and recognize what the movements are before they are asked to justify them. |

| | |
|---|---|
| • Your teacher will explain that the Action Narration technique means that each of the characters can clap his/her hands when they want to freeze the action, allowing them to Action Narrate what they are going to do and/or say next, and why. The aim is that no one moves or speaks without revealing their motives and they must always freeze the action by clapping their hands before they do this. | |
| • You will be working in a small group of three or four students. Each group is given an extract from either Act 2 Scene 10 or Scene 15. Use the Action Narration technique to explore your extract, thinking carefully about what motivates the characters at every stage. Continue the action-narrated scene until you reach the end of your extract and all the characters have revealed their motives for their actions and speech. | The scene can be divided into different size extracts depending on the size of the class.

The use of Action Narration has a direct effect on the students' understanding of the play in performance. |
| • The Action Narrated scenes can be shared with the whole class and/or presented as Rolling Theatre. | Position the groups around the room according to the order of the extracts they were given. |

## Additional activities, analysis and/or discussion

1. Discuss what roles the playwright, actor or director have in revealing and/or deciding on the characters' motivations. How do they achieve this?

2. How does this Action Narration activity help you to develop an understanding of the playwright's techniques? What skills are required?

3. Discuss the two daughter/father relationships explored in Act 2 Scenes 10 and 15 and how these relate to the roles of Gemma and Kate in the play.

4. Return to the Role on the Object (box and stick) for Gemma and Kate from Activity 3 and the motorway bridge diagram from Activity 5 to help explore Act 2 Scenes 10 and 15 and the techniques used by the playwright to present the characters and their journeys.

# 8 It's Not Many Times In Life You Get A Chance To Do Something Like This

Investigate and analyse the script by exploring a specific character and the playwright's techniques in developing her role in the play.

| Learning and Teaching | Guidance and Resources |
|---|---|
| • Sit in a large semicircle and watch the short film clip about the foot-and-mouth outbreak. Discuss the contents of the clip and how it relates to the play. | Resources – various YouTube clips about the foot-and-mouth outbreak are available or see BBC Rewind: The 2001 foot-and-mouth outbreak<br><br>www.oxfordsecondary.co.uk/ cowgirloxfordplayscripts |
| • You will be working in a small group of between three and six students. Each group is given an extract from the play (see extracts below).<br><br>**Extract 1 (two people)**: (pages 49–51)<br>*From* What's wrong, it's going well<br>*to* Stupid boys.<br><br>**Extract 2 (five people)**: (pages 51–53)<br>*From* Gemma!<br>*to* And that was the lot.<br><br>**Extract 3 (three people)**: (pages 53–55)<br>*From* Good day at school, was it?<br>*to* …we could go to Gran's if you fancied a bingo night.<br><br>**Extract 4 (five/six people)**: (pages 56–57)<br>*From* Go away! I'm feeding Donna.<br>*to* I'll tell her.<br><br>**Extract 5 (Teacher to read)**: (page 57–60)<br>Act 2 Scenes 10 and 11<br><br>**Extract 6 (four/five people)**: (pages 60–61)<br>*From* I got on my bike and cycled back to Gran's.<br>*to* I don't want to feel that any more. | Copies of the scripts can be used for this activity but the teacher might find it useful to reproduce the extracts on sheets of A4 paper or card. If these are colour-coded, it is easy for the teacher to see which of the extracts different groups are working on and the chronological order can more easily be maintained.<br><br>By exploring these extracts, the students begin to select and analyse information from the text. They also begin to take a real interest in the material and want to know more. By Action Reading the extracts, they have to consider some of the initial issues that directors and actors need to address. |

| | |
|---|---|
| **Extract 7 (two people)**: (page 62)<br>*From* First lesson.<br>*to* That was beautiful.<br><br>**Extract 8 (five people)**: (pages 62–64)<br>*From* I felt good, like everything was going to be all right.<br>*to* No! | During the time that students are 'rehearsing' their Digital Video Clips, the teacher will need to stop them at regular intervals to focus on the Still Images and the ways that character, use of space and tension are being explored. |
| • In your group, produce a short Digital Video Clip of your extract. (For a reminder of the Digital Video Clip process, see Activity 3, page 93.)<br><br>• The film clip, seen at the start of this activity, will be shown in between the Digital Video Clips and might, therefore, influence the way that you present your extract and/or the emphasis that you give to particular words or actions. | After a few minutes of 'rehearsal' stop the students (by counting them down from 5 to 1) and ask them to show the Still Images. |
| • As a class, produce your Digital Video Clips as Rolling Theatre. | Make sure that the groups are positioned around the room in the correct order. Play the film clip before, in between and at the end of the Digital Video Clips. |
| • In your group, use the information you have gained from producing the Digital Video Clip of your extract to select what you feel is the most important line from the extract. Present a Still Image that illustrates this line and defines the important issues and ideas at this stage in the play. The Still Image can be a literal or symbolic interpretation of the line.<br><br>• Write the line on a large sheet of paper and place it in front of your Still Image. Think about how the line might be said while holding the Still Image. For example, would it be said by one character or in chorus? Would it be echoed or whispered? | The process might need to be modelled first with the teacher and class discussing one of the extracts and deciding how the line could be presented either symbolically or literally.<br><br><br><br><br><br>Resources – large sheets of paper and pens |

| | |
|---|---|
| ● Now create a Still Image to represent what Gran would think or feel if she observed that particular moment. Would she see and hear what is actually taking place or would she see something different?<br><br>● As a group, discuss what Gran's thoughts would be at this moment. Write down Gran's thoughts, in the first person (using 'I'), and place it in front of the Still Image. As with the line that accompanied the first Still Image in this activity, think about how Gran's thoughts might be said out loud while holding the second Still Image. What tone or emphasis might be used? | This process might also need to be modelled first with the teacher and class discussing one of the lines and deciding how Gran might interpret that moment and what her thoughts might be. |
| ● As a class, produce your Still Images, accompanying lines of text and Gran's thoughts as Rolling Theatre. Music is used to guide you. All the groups freeze in their initial Still Image. The first group speaks their line from the script and then gradually merges from their first Still Image into the Image that presents what Gran 'sees'. Then they speak Gran's thoughts. Once they have finished, the next group knows that they can begin, saying their line, merging into the second Still Image and speaking Gran's thoughts. This continues until all the groups have merged from one Still Image to the other and spoken the text and thoughts. | Walk through the process with one group to model the activity to the whole class.<br><br>Play music (e.g. Bach flute works) or sections of the foot-and-mouth film clips before and in between each Still Image and accompanying speech. |

## Additional activities, analysis and/or discussion

1. Discuss the techniques that the playwright has used to present aspects of the play through different characters' eyes. How is the role of the 'observer' linked to the audience's role throughout the play?

2. When Kate describes the foot-and-mouth outbreak to Gemma, she says, 'There's times I can still smell it.' Discuss what she means by this and how the issues in the past about foot-and-mouth relate to other problems/ideas in the play. Immediately following this, and after Kate says 'He tries hard, my dad', Gemma tells Kate about her dad being in prison. Why?

# 9 You Don't Know What It's Like

Explore and analyse the ways that the playwright develops tension in the play and interpret the characters' thoughts and motivations.

| Learning and Teaching | Guidance and Resources |
|---|---|
| • As a class, read Act 2 Scenes 17 and 18. Return to the Role on the Object technique (from Activity 3) to explore Gemma's character. Identify from your understanding of the play so far what you now know about Gemma. Place your word on or near the box, thinking carefully where you might place it. Discuss what changes have been made to the Role on the Object since the start of the play and what motivates Gemma. | If different coloured cards are used each time the Role on the Object activity is undertaken, then the changes can be tracked throughout and discussion can take place about how the playwright presents the characters on a 'journey'.<br><br>Prop – box |
| • Sit in a large semicircle facing the projected text of Act 2 Scenes 16, 17 and 18 (pages 67–68):<br><br>*From* So I went back, across the bridge and up the hill.<br><br>*to* You lost? | Project the text. |
| • A member of the class is given the role of Gemma and the teacher adopts the role of Mr Mostyn. Sculpt them into the scene at this point. You will need to consider their frozen positions, facial expressions and gestures. Other members of the class might adjust the positions until a final Sculpture is agreed. | Give value to the different positions offered by explaining that the director at different points in the scene could have used the positions. Ensure that the sculpted positions are supported with evidence from the text. |

- You will now be working in groups of three or four students. Your teacher will allocate the name of one character from the play to your group. Drawing on your knowledge of your character's relationship with Gemma and his/her role in the play, develop, as a group, a speech, in the first person, that they might deliver to Gemma at this moment to help her confront Mr Mostyn. You will be Informing the Dialogue that takes place between Gemma and Mr Mostyn. As a group, you need to decide who will say what and how the speech is said.

- To accompany the speech, you also need to prepare a Still Image in your group that symbolically represents your character's view of Gemma and his/her feelings about what she is about to do and what she should say to Mr Mostyn.

- Return to the sculpted characters at the moment when Mr Mostyn says, 'You lost?'. Gemma turns away from Mr Mostyn to face the groups of students that have been positioned around her in their Still Images (see an example below).

Resources – character cards (Gran, Mam, Darren, Mr Banerjee, Morris, Sian, Karuna, Mr Thomas)

By preparing speeches, the groups will inform the dialogue and, therefore, analyse the techniques used by the playwright and Gemma's motivation.

Position the groups around the sculpted scene as shown in the diagram below.

When Gemma turns away from Mr Mostyn, the teacher can come out of role to explain how the speeches and Informed Dialogue will be presented.

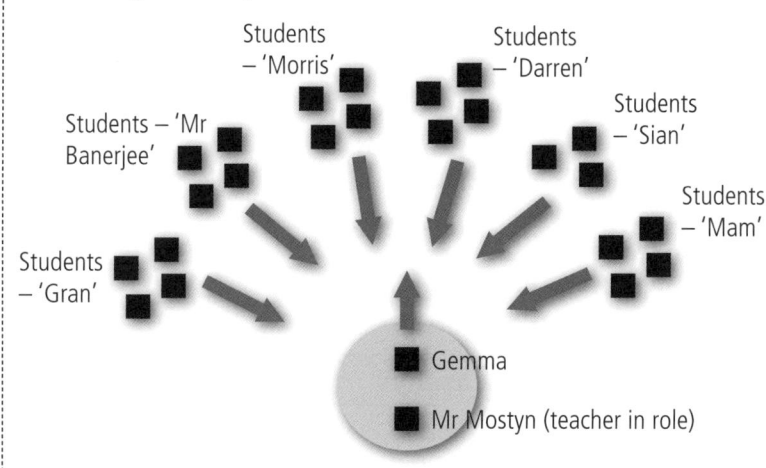

| | |
|---|---|
| • As a class, produce your Still Images and speeches as Rolling Theatre. All the groups freeze in their initial Still Image and then the first group unfreezes, completes their speech and then freezes again. This continues until all groups have delivered their speeches. | Play music at the start, end and in between each speech.<br><br>Remind students of the nature of Spect-acting and the importance of freezing in the final Still Images at the end of the Rolling Theatre. |
| • Gemma will then turn to the Teacher in Role as Mr Mostyn who will repeat the line 'You lost?' The two sculpted characters will then continue the conversation. Gemma's responses and comments to Mr Mostyn will be informed by the speeches she has just listened to and the teacher will also use comments, as well as statements directly from the script. At times there will be silences and, if needed, the students representing the other characters can repeat a line of their speech to 'inform' Gemma of what to say next. The dialogue between Gemma and Mr Mostyn will continue until the Teacher in Role as Mr Mostyn turns away from her. Gemma then turns back to the student groups and reads from the projected text from the script:<br>**You put Mr Thomas under pressure. Kate was only trying to save the cows. She cares, is all. If you were a cow you'd be well dead and eaten by now. My gran needs that cow and so does everyone else. You don't, you got loads. You don't live on the Mawr. You don't know what it's like. You haven't got a clue. 'Miser Mostyn' they call you – no wonder.<br>I screamed all the way down the hill.** (page 69) | The teacher will need to be familiar with the arguments that Mr Mostyn uses in Act 2 Scene 18 so that he/she can introduce them into the dialogue. Mr Mostyn's responses can also be informed by the characters' speeches so that particular ideas and issues can be brought up to provoke a response from Gemma.<br><br><br>Project the text. |

## Additional activities, analysis and/or discussion

1. Discuss what techniques the playwright has used to develop tension throughout the play and to explore the influences that the different characters have on each other.

2. Explore how Activity 9 might help an actor prepare for the staging of this scene in the play and/or the playwright to write the scene.

3. As a class, read Act 2 Scene 18. Analyse how the language devices and dramatic techniques are used to explore characters, relationships, power and tension in this scene and other moments in the play.

# 10 WHAT'S ALL THIS ABOUT?

Explore the adaptation process and analyse the novelist's and playwright's techniques.

| Learning and Teaching | Guidance and Resources |
|---|---|
| ● Sit in a large semicircle facing the projected text. Read the extract from the novel which explores the events of the night Gemma returns from Mr Mostyn's:<br><br>**As soon as I got in they asked me how it went. "Fine," I said. "He was angry, of course." I didn't want to tell them Kate's dad had said he'd take them straight to be killed, 'specially as I saw Gran and Darren looking so hopeful. They told me everyone had agreed taking them on to the Common was a good plan, apart from Roger. I realised that this time tomorrow all the cows might be on their way to the slaughterhouse, and all because of my big mouth. That night I sat at the top of the stairs and listened to Mam talking on the phone. "Well, she takes after me, Robbie ... says it how it is... You should've called earlier – she's in bed now... Scared, are you? It's strange, Rob, but things are different round here. Everyone says it's because of the cows. I don't know. All I can say is that it's different..." When she hung up I watched her. She took out a cigarette and put it in her mouth. She picked up her lighter, then she stopped, sighed and pulled the cigarette out. Her head dropped back against the settee. I went quietly downstairs. "What are you doing out of bed?" she asked. "Thirsty, Mam – really thirsty." I went into the kitchen. "Want some water?" "No."** | Project the text. |

**I filled and emptied a glass a few times, then I took a sip and went to the doorway of the lounge. Mam was staring at nothing. I walked to the settee and sat beside her. My heart was pounding. I thought she might tell me to go back upstairs, but I wanted to be with her. I sipped at the water and Mam didn't say anything. We both just sat there staring at the TV that was off. I remembered sitting on that settee snuggled up to her. It was so long ago it felt like a dream.** (pages 199–200)

- As a whole class, stand in a large circle. One member of the class is given the role of Mam and another member of the class is given the role of Gemma. Sculpt them (in the centre of the circle) into the scene at this point. You will need to consider their frozen positions and facial expressions. Other members of the class might adjust the positions until a final sculpture is agreed.

Ensure that the sculpted positions are supported with evidence from the text. Give value to the different positions offered by explaining that at different points in the scene these could have been seen.

Project the text.

- The teacher will choose a student to take the role of the 'Writer' (Giancarlo Gemin). Place the Writer in the Sculpted Image where you think he should be. You might use various criteria for this, including the writer's distance from the character, the empathy created, the events and the writer's intention. Justify your choices, using evidence from the text to support your ideas.

- Discuss the positioning as a class. Throughout this discussion, other students should demonstrate the position they feel is most appropriate by moving and Placing the Writer and then justifying their choice.

Ask specific questions such as 'Is the writer looking through Gemma's eyes or at her?' or 'How close is the writer to the character in terms of empathy or the sympathy created?'

It is important that the students physically move the Writer, before justifying why.

- Another member of the class is given the role of the 'Reader'. Position the reader in the frozen scene where you think he/she should be. You might use various criteria for this, including the reader's distance from the character, the empathy felt, the events and the reader's understanding of a particular idea. Justify your choice, using evidence from the text to support your ideas.

It should be clear that there is no 'right' answer. Students are developing their understanding of the writer's techniques and perspective through the arguments and evidence that are presented.

| | |
|---|---|
| • As a class, discuss the positioning of the Reader. Throughout this discussion, other students should demonstrate the position they feel is most appropriate by moving and Placing the Reader and then justifying their choice. | Students should be encouraged to quote from the text to support their arguments. |
| • Read the next line of the novel, '"That was your dad on the phone,"she said.' (page 200) | |
| • As a class, read the following extract from the play, from the start of Act 2 Scene 19 (page 69): *From At home. Late.* *to* Your dad was on the phone. Discuss why you think the playwright chose to begin the scene when he did and not include Gemma overhearing the conversation on the phone. | Project the text. Students should be encouraged to compare specific aspects of the two texts and the different techniques the writers have used. |
| • Members of the class are given the roles of Mam and Gemma. Sculpt them into the scene at this moment, as described above. | Again, ensure that the positioning is supported with evidence from the text. |
| • Another student is chosen to be the 'Playwright' (Mike Kenny). Position or Place the Playwright in the frozen scene where you think he should be. • Discuss the positioning as a class. Throughout the discussion, other students should demonstrate the position they feel is most appropriate by moving and Placing the Playwright and justifying their choice. Discuss whether this differs from the position of the Writer placed earlier. Why? • A student representing the 'Audience' can now be placed in the same way. Discuss what differences there are between Placing the Reader and Placing the Audience. Discuss what these differences might tell us about the adaptation process. | Discuss any differences in the position of the Playwright compared with that of the Writer. What reasons are there for this? When Placing the Audience it is important that it is placed in terms of perspective, empathy and effect rather than a literal positioning in relation to the theatre space. |

- The student, who represented the Writer (novelist Giancarlo Gemin) earlier, should stand at the side of the frozen scene. Should the Writer (Giancarlo Gemin) be placed into this scene from the script and, if so, where? Does the original writer remain part of the play? Are they left outside the scene? Are they near to the Playwright (Mike Kenny) or do they have a different perspective? Position/Place the Writer where you feel it is most appropriate for him to be.

  Specific examples can be used here to show where writers have remained involved in the adaptation process and where they have completely handed it over.

- Read and discuss the comments by Giancarlo Gemin, the novelist, and Mike Kenny, the playwright.

> This was one of my favourite scenes in the book. It's about that moment when people reveal their deepest feelings. That's what Gemma does when, for the first time, she realises the difficult position her mother is in.
>
> When Gemma goes back upstairs I had to stay with her because she is the narrator (first-person perspective), but in the play the audience get to see Gemma's mother's reaction to what her daughter has said. It will be a powerful moment. Mother and daughter have come back together; bridges are re-built and we know something good has taken place.
>
> *Giancarlo Gemin*

This was one of my favourite scenes in the novel. I love the economy in it: the image of Mam, tired and worn out, and the quiet affection between Mam and Gemma. However, theatre works in a different way to a novel. A novelist can tell you what a character is thinking. A playwright has to show you. (I know that's not strictly true. A character can directly talk to the audience, and Gemma does do it in the play, but it can get boring. Plus, part of the way a play works is that the audience is given the job of working out what is going on inside the characters. It's the way an audience uses its imagination.) And a playwright's main tool is dialogue, people talking to each other. In this scene in the book, there is virtually no talk, but you know exactly what is going on.

There's a rule in writing for theatre: go into a scene as late as possible. You have only a very little time to make a scene work and an actor always carries with them the atmosphere and thoughts from the previous scene. I felt I needed to follow Gemma straight out of the previous argument with Mostyn, into seeing Mam. It means she's still angry and it hasn't been softened by overhearing Mam's phone call with Dad. Then when she asks the question about Sian and Gary Tobin, '…have I got an angry sort of face? Like Sian and Gary Tobin?' it has a real edge. In the book, she has had the realisation about them earlier, so we know what she's getting at. In the play this is our one chance.

*Mike Kenny*

117

| Additional activities, analysis and/or discussion |
| --- |
| **1.** Discuss the different techniques used by the novelist and playwright in this scene. |
| **2.** Discuss the different approaches/techniques used by the playwright and novelist to explore the characters and the relationships between them. |
| **3.** Return to the Role on the Object (box and stick) for Gemma and Kate from Activity 3 and the motorway bridge diagram from Activity 5 to help explore Act 2 Scene 19 and the techniques used by the playwright to present the characters and their journeys. |
| **4.** As a class, read and discuss Act 2 Scenes 19 to 24 before moving on to the next activity. |

# 11 I COULDN'T WORK IT OUT AT FIRST

Explore the ending of the play and analyse the techniques used to draw the ideas together and present the changes that have taken place.

| Learning and Teaching | Guidance and Resources |
| --- | --- |
| • Projected on to the screen/wall is the image of the place used in Activity 1. As a class, read the opening of Act 2 Scene 24 (pages 80–81):<br><br>*From* The one person missing was the Cowgirl herself.<br><br>*to* … snaking all the way up Craig-y-Nos Hill. | Project the Image used in Activity 1. |
| • One member of the class is given the role of Gemma and another member of the class is given the role of Kate. Sculpt Gemma and Kate in the scene at this point in front of the projected image. The rest of the class should be arranged in a large semicircle and Gemma and Kate should be facing them, holding a bucket between them. | Resource – bucket |

| | |
|---|---|
| ● Your teacher will give you a milk carton and a line that Gemma or Kate speaks towards the end of the play. | Resources – milk cartons filled with artificial coins; lines of text<br><br>Depending on the size of the class, divide up the text from, 'Hope they're not all expecting a cup of tea' to 'The holy herdsman' so that each student has a line or phrase to read. |
| ● As music plays quietly in the background, the first student walks clockwise in a large circle towards Gemma and Kate. The first student should be followed by a line of students so that the whole circle moves clockwise towards the two sculpted characters of Kate and Gemma. | Play music throughout the activity. |
| ● As the first student passes Gemma and Kate, he/she says his/her line, 'Hope they're not all expecting' out loud and empties the contents of his/her carton into the bucket. The next student, passing in front of Gemma and Kate then says his/her phrase, 'a cup of tea' and empties the contents of his/her carton into the bucket, before continuing around an imaginary large circle to return to his/her original place. The process continues until all the students have said their lines, emptied the contents of the cartons into the bucket and returned to their place in the semicircle. | The lines are spoken in the order they appear in the script. |
| ● The teacher then reads the end of the play.<br><br>*From* **Gemma** *and* **Kate** *pull away.* **Gemma** *has her bike.*<br><br>*to Off they go. Screaming.* | |

## Additional activities, analysis and/or discussion

1. Why did the playwright choose to end the play in this way?

2. Discuss the techniques used by the novelist and playwright that make this scene particularly powerful.

3. Discuss, and evidence, the dramatic techniques and theatrical devices used in the final scene. How do these devices influence our understanding of the narrative, characters and ideas?

# 12 You've All Changed So Much

Identify key moments in the play and our response to them and reflect on the techniques used to ensure that these moments have impact.

| Learning and Teaching | Guidance and Resources |
|---|---|
| • As a class, or individually, recap on the ideas and techniques explored throughout the play so far. | Look back through all the activities to help this process. |
| • Projected on to the screen/wall is the image of the place used in Activity 1. However, this time a simple grid reference system has been superimposed on to it so that particular places on the image can be identified. | Project the image of the map with grid references.<br><br>www.oxfordsecondary.co.uk/ cowgirloxfordplayscripts |
| • You will be working in a small group of three or four students. Reflecting on the whole play and all the activities that you have been involved in, identify as a group a significant line, word, drama technique or action that has had an impact on you. You are going to present this as a Still Image (with speech) or short Digital Video Clip. | The students will need time to discuss all the different activities and significant lines from the play. They will also need time to develop and rehearse the Still Image/Digital Video Clip. |
| • Once you have chosen the line or technique, identify a place on the projected image that you would associate it with. Write the grid reference for that location on a large piece of paper and place it on the floor in front of your Still Image/Digital Video Clip. | Groups should be spread out around the room and, if possible, reflect the positionings and grid references on the projected image.<br><br>Resources – large pieces of paper and pens |

| | |
|---|---|
| • As a class, produce your Still Images/Digital Video Clips as Rolling Theatre. The order of the groups is this time, however, determined by the grid reference that the teacher calls out and points to on the image. | Play music before and in between each Still Image/ Digital Video Clip. |
| • All the groups freeze in their initial Still Image and then the teacher will call out a grid reference and point to it on the map. The group with that grid reference unfreezes, completes the reading or speech and then freezes again. When they freeze, the teacher calls out another grid reference. This continues with all the groups producing their Digital Video Clip, until all groups have shown their pieces. | Remind students of the nature of Spect-acting and the importance of freezing in the final Still Images at the end of the Rolling Theatre. |
| • When you are not presenting your Digital Video Clip, you can become a Spect-actor. You should remain in your place, in order for all the groups to freeze in their final Still Image at the end. | |

## Additional activities, analysis and/or discussion

1. Discuss how the drama activities have contributed to the development of analytical skills. How might these skills, activities and ideas be transferred to unfamiliar texts or writers?

2. Analyse how the language devices and dramatic techniques are used throughout the activities and by the playwright to explore characters, relationships, a sense of voice, power and tension.

# 13 You Can't Go Back

Develop critical thinking and be able to analyse techniques and their effects, supported by evidence from the text.

| Learning and Teaching | Guidance and Resources |
|---|---|
| • Sit in a large circle. In the centre of the circle is the box used throughout the activities. | Prop – box (to represent Gemma's jewellery box) with artificial leaves inside |

| | |
|---|---|
| • The sound effect of traffic is played in the background. | Sound effects – traffic sounds (motorway) are used throughout this activity. |
| • The teacher picks up the box and passes it to one of the students, opening it so that the leaves inside can be seen. | |
| • The teacher will give each student a leaf-shaped piece of paper, or artificial leaf and a pen. Thinking carefully about the play as a whole, decide what you think the playwright wants the audience to take away with them from the play. Write this on the leaf. | Resources – leaf-shaped pieces of paper/artificial leaves and pens |
| • The box is passed round the circle again as each student reads out what they have written on their leaf and then places it in the box. | |
| • The teacher takes the box and reads the final line of the play (page 82): **'We could go anywhere. Hold on tight!'** He/she then turns the box upside down and scatters the leaves on the floor as the sound of traffic continues and eventually fades. | Project the text. |

## Additional activities, analysis and/or discussion

1. Discuss the significance of the changes made to Activity 2 during the final activity.

2. What are the key images/lines/ideas that remain in the audience's mind after the play has ended?

3. Using all the evidence, information and analysis developed throughout the work, prepare an analytical response to the text as a whole. For example, you could prepare a response to the following statement: '*Cowgirl* is a play that explores the sense of community and the journeys that individuals within that community go on to move from fear to empathy. Discuss the techniques the playwright uses to explore the characters' and the audience's journeys throughout the play.'